FLORY

A Miraculous Story of Survival

Flory A. Van Beek

HarperOne
An Imprint of HarperCollins*Publishers*

HarperOne

A version of this book was published by Seven Locks Press in 1998.

FLORY: *A Miraculous Story of Survival*. Copyright © 2008 by Flory A. Van Beek. All rights reserved. Printed in the United States of America. No part of this book may be used or reproduced in any manner whatsoever without written permission except in the case of brief quotations embodied in critical articles and reviews. For information address HarperCollins Publishers, 10 East 53rd Street, New York, NY 10022.

HarperCollins®, 🏛®, and HarperOne™ are trademarks of HarperCollins Publishers.

Interior design: Laura Lind Design

ISBN 978–0–06–117614–2

Book Club Edition

*I have written this testimonial in the sacred memory
of my beloved mother and all family members who perished
at the hands of the German Nazis in the greatest human
tragedy the world has ever known.*

*In the Jewish faith it is unbearable to think that the names
of deceased ones have been blotted out without knowing
where they perished and where they are buried.*

*It is my fervent wish that with this testimonial their blessed
memories will live on through future generations, though
their hopes and dreams were brutally destroyed.*

*This book will also serve as a tribute to the gracious people,
total strangers, who gave us shelter in the most dangerous
of circumstances. They showed extraordinary courage and
risked their own lives in the face of the enemy.*

*In memoriam of my siblings Ies (and Elisabeth)
Cohen, Ben Cohen, Elisabeth Cohen-Coster, and
my mother-in-law Jette Aufhauser.*

Contents

Note from the Author

When I immigrated to America from Holland, in 1948, I brought with me a huge suitcase filled with close to one thousand documents, diaries, newspaper clippings and photographs, all of which I had saved during the five-year war and Holocaust. They had been hidden by me in metal boxes and were buried deep in the ground, with the help of our benefactors and with whom we were hidden. This book is based on these documents.

Each time that I looked at that suitcase, filled with its dismal contents, I got pangs in my stomach, thinking how my darling mother found her death in the gas chambers of Sobibor and how she must have suffered.

As a testimonial and everlasting memory to my mother, I wanted to bring tribute to her life by writing this manuscript, which I began thirty years ago. The emotions of the past overwhelmed me to such an extent, that I burst out in tears again and again. After my first attempt, I cried so bitterly that my husband Felix said "Stop, I want you to stop for now and I will put the suitcase somewhere so you will no longer see it." It is said that time heals, but it does not. One learns to cope with tragedy a bit better.

We moved to Newport Beach, California, in 1962, and I began to write again looking out from my room to palm trees and lovely greenery with cheerful flowers. Every word and every event in this publication is true. To my amazement, when initially published in Holland and elsewhere, it became a success. I finally have learned to accept the past, knowing that my mother is at rest in the Heavens with the Angels, and in her memory I consider this book a decent grave and epitaph.

Acknowledgments

This book is meant to be my Eulogy for my dear mother's unknown grave located in a strange land, where she met her tragic death in such an abominable way. It has been written in tears. Through the support and love of my dear husband Felix and many friends, I received the strength to continue writing. Now it is time for me to express my sincere thanks to those involved in the publishing of my testimonial. First, my gratitude goes to our dear friend Jim Riordan, for his initial assistance in constructing this book. My profound thanks to my very active and enthusiastic literary representatives and film producers Daniel Sladek and Chris Taaffe, who championed my life story "this close" to being produced as a major miniseries at ABC. Despite a setback due to extraordinarily unfortunate circumstances, the project is still in development with their company, and I am convinced it will make its way onto film in the near future. My sincere thanks to Eileen Cope and the team at Trident Media Group for their hard work on my behalf, and to HarperOne staff members Gideon Weil, Cynthia DiTiberio, and Laurie Dunne. My profound appreciation and thanks to all those from my home country of Holland for your fan letters and gifts, including flags!

Sincerely,
Flory A. Van Beek

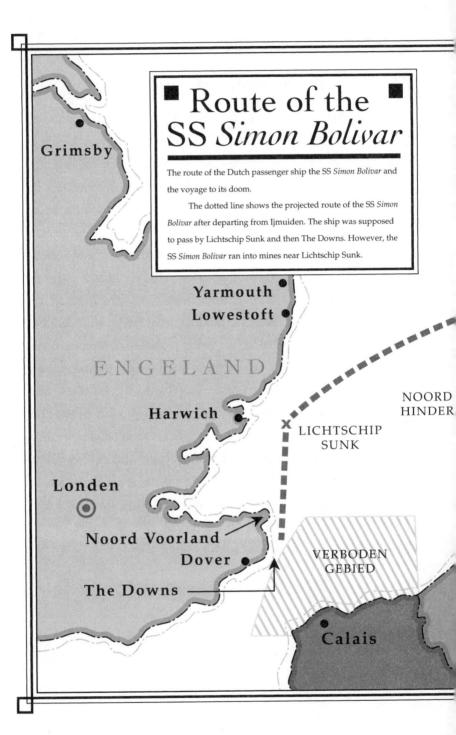

Route of the SS *Simon Bolivar*

The route of the Dutch passenger ship the SS *Simon Bolivar* and the voyage to its doom.

The dotted line shows the projected route of the SS *Simon Bolivar* after departing from Ijmuiden. The ship was supposed to pass by Lichtschip Sunk and then The Downs. However, the SS *Simon Bolivar* ran into mines near Lichtschip Sunk.

Grimsby

Yarmouth
Lowestoft

ENGELAND

Harwich

NOORD HINDER

LICHTSCHIP SUNK

Londen

Noord Voorland

Dover

VERBODEN GEBIED

The Downs

Calais

CHAPTER I

The Early Years

Amersfoort

"You can take your skates along with you today," I heard my mother say as I was preparing for school.

My family lived in a small town in the Netherlands, the country of my birth. The town was called Amersfoort, located in the center of Holland. Amersfoort was quite picturesque, surrounded by many canals, old castles, and lush forests. In the winter, when the canals were frozen and the ice was strong, children could go to school on their ice skates, taking shortcuts and having lots of fun at the same time.

I was the youngest of four children, born of Jewish parents in the city of Rotterdam. My oldest brother, Jes (Ies), was nineteen years my senior. Then came my brother Ben, ten years older than I, followed by my sister, Elisabeth, who was nine years older. When I was very young my family lived in Rotterdam, close to my father's parents, sisters, and brothers. It was a large family. Many Sunday mornings when all of us assembled at my grandparents' home, we had to wait in line to pay our respects to my grandmother. My grandfather had passed away long before.

My mother was very beautiful; she had married my father when she was nineteen. She was soft-spoken, gentle, and an attentive listener. When I was five years old my father died in an accident, leaving my mother devastated. It was then that she decided to move to Amersfoort to be near her parents and siblings.

My mother's parents, my beloved grandparents Oma and Opa, were very religious and helped to raise me in the Orthodox Jewish fashion. When I turned six years old I began Hebrew school and shortly thereafter learned to read Hebrew.

My school, called De Meisjes School, was an all-girls' school located on a plateau near an old castle. My teachers were quite strict; the headmistress especially was to be awed and feared. However, all who attended De Meisjes School received an excellent education, including learning the languages of our neighboring countries. In the fourth grade we started to learn French, followed by English in the fifth grade and German in the sixth grade. I disliked mathematics but loved languages, which were taught, as was the custom, by teachers from the countries where these languages were spoken.

I attended school each day from nine in the morning until noon and from two to four in the afternoon, with the exception of Wednesdays and Saturdays. On Wednesdays we attended school half a day, and I did not go to school on Saturdays, which was the Holy Sabbath. On the Sabbath I went with my grandfather, Opa, to the synagogue. This was an exciting event because afterward my sister and I went home to join my mother, grandmother, aunts, and uncles for a plentiful luncheon. We sang Hebrew songs of grace and enjoyed sweets, and I savored the feeling of safety and security with my family in this warm and loving atmosphere.

Opa was very handsome and dignified looking. On our way to the synagogue, people greeted him with reverence. One of my favorite memories from this time is my grandfather reading the daily newspaper aloud to my grandmother, whose eyes were not in good condition. The love they shared between them was enviable.

My birthday was celebrated on St. Nicolaas Day, December 5, although my real birthday is December 3. St. Nicolaas Day (in Dutch, Sinterklaas Dag) is always celebrated in Holland with much joy and fun and many surprises. Legend has it that St. Nicolaas arrives on a ship from Spain and, after disembarking, mounts a white horse. With his Moorish helpers, he visits schools and homes in the township. No matter what religion one observed, Sinterklaas Dag was celebrated by all.

So on this particular day, skating home, I was very much looking forward to Sinterklaas Dag, birthday presents, and my school's upcoming chorale presentation. However, as I approached my home, a funny feeling came over me that I couldn't explain. All through my life I would experience this feeling again and again as a warning of impending doom.

My mother greeted me at the door with tears streaming down her face. She took me in her arms, and as she held me my sister, who stood nearby, said, "Opa died."

"What do you mean?" I said. "Opa cannot die." But I had lost my beloved grandfather.

The funeral was attended by all who knew him: dignitaries, friends, family, neighbors. The mourning period lasted seven days, and during that time people would come in and out of my grandparents' house with food—especially egg dishes because eggs were regarded as the symbol of life.

After my grandfather died I watched my grandmother gradually deteriorate. Within a half year she too passed away.

After the death of my grandparents in Amersfoort, my mother became increasingly nervous. We ended up selling our house and moving to Amsterdam, where my brother Ben was living. It was a tremendous change for our family, moving from a small town to a big city. I was enrolled in the Joseph Israels H.B.S., a school named for the famous painter who lived from 1824 to 1911.

I soon adjusted to these changes and came to enjoy school. Music had always been very important in our family, and the schools of higher learning offered a fantastic program that included free musical concerts once or twice each month.

Before these concerts the principal violinist would visit our class to explain the repertoire. He would discuss the composers, the interpretation of the music, the instruments, the dynamics. When my class attended the concerts I would listen attentively, understanding and recognizing all I had learned from the principal violinist.

During these school years I spent my summer vacations with my oldest brother and his wife back in Amersfoort. My brother and his wife were a devoted couple but had no children. They lived in a modest home, which was a haven of warmth and coziness. They always catered to me and made my stay with them a happy time.

And so, between school, sports, music, and the fun of growing up, my three years in Amsterdam went by very quickly. I grew up under the reign of Queen Wilhelmina Oranje Van Nassau, who was popular among the seven million Dutch people during that time. But there is nothing more permanent than change. Just as I approached my fifteenth birthday, my family was notified that my paternal grandmother had passed away in Rotterdam. My whole family attended her funeral. She had reached a ripe old age, but it was sad for me because now, with the death of this grandmother, I had lost all of the grandparents I loved so much.

After my grandmother's death, and the proper mourning period that followed, we stayed with my father's large family in Rotterdam for a while and became reacquainted with our many aunts, uncles, and cousins. One day the oldest brother of my father, my Uncle Saam, asked to speak with us. He was an impressive, stern-looking man who did not mince words. Although he did not speak much, he always started or ended each sentence with, roughly translated from the Dutch, "you see" or "don't you see."

In spite of his stern countenance, there was kindness in his eyes, and his opinion was worthy of our trust. He first looked at my mother and said, "You see, now that you are more acquainted with all of the family, I'd like to see you permanently come back to live in Rotterdam." My mother, shy as she was, looked a bit confused and sorrowful. He continued, looking at me now, "You see, your father would have wanted me to be your guardian, and I think it would be best to enroll you in a school where you will continue with languages and learn more practical skills, don't you see. I will be responsible for the two of you and give you advice on everything, you see." My mother nodded shyly, and my uncle ended the conversation with, "I don't like to see you move so much; you need more stability, don't you see?"

And so my mother and I moved back to Rotterdam that year. My sister lived in the country with a family for whom she worked. My brothers continued to live in Amersfoort and Amsterdam.

My mother rented a modest apartment in the center of Rotterdam and enrolled me in a school that specialized in languages and practical arts. This was a good time for my mother and me. Our family was supportive and loving, and my uncle kept his word to us and was generous with good advice. Although my father's side of the family was not religious, my mother could not forget her religious ties with her parents. So my mother and I frequently went to the synagogue and never missed services on the High Holy Days.

About this time I began to bloom, and when I was fifteen my mother enrolled me in a Jewish youth club, the JJK. This club offered many activities, including tennis, sailing, swimming, and ballet. In addition, through this club I attended lectures and book reviews by renowned speakers. I made a lot of friends, and with the approval of our parents we often went by car to the Kurhaus, a fine music hall in the resort town of Scheveningen, on the North Sea.

But nothing lasts forever, it seems. By that time many Jewish families from Germany had settled in Holland. My mother began to talk about Hitler and how his burgeoning power would affect the Jewish population. But she always ended these discussions with "But nothing will happen in Holland because the queen is here. And Holland always stays neutral."

CHAPTER 2

Storm Clouds Rising

With my mother before leaving Holland

The Netherlands is so called because it is located below sea level on the North Sea. With Germany to the east, Denmark to the north, and Belgium, Luxembourg, and France to the south, the Netherlands is a place of many languages, and my family became quite familiar with all of them.

My ancestors had lived in Holland since the beginning of the seventeenth century, and Jews had settled in Holland long before that. In the fifteenth and sixteenth centuries thousands of Spanish and Portuguese Jews fled to Holland to escape the Spanish Inquisition and were lovingly welcomed by the Dutch. These Sephardic (Spanish) Jews brought much trade to Holland, a welcome development. In later years some streets in Holland were named after these Jews, who had contributed so much to the economy. The Portuguese Jews who settled in Holland built a beautiful synagogue in Amsterdam, which is still in use. They also produced great philosophers, writers, painters, and scientists, all of whom added much culture to Holland.

In 1806 Holland was occupied by King Louis, brother of Napoleon. The Jewish people under his reign enjoyed freedom of religion but were required to take surnames. Historically, Jews had been given only first names, being known as, for example, "so-and-so, son of, or daughter of." During this time in Holland they were required to take on a last name, and most Jews chose the name of their profession or the name of a street or a canal.

During that time also, many French words and expressions entered the Dutch language. For example, the Dutch motto, "Je Maintiendrai," is French for "I shall maintain." This motto appears on all military and police uniforms and dates back to when Louis Bonaparte was king of Holland, from 1806 to 1810.

As Jews, we felt more than secure living in Holland under the reign of Queen Wilhelmina. I cannot recall any hint of anti-Semitism during the time of my youth, although Hitler was gaining in power.

One day in 1935 my mother said, "We have to take in and help a German family." I did not quite understand the situation at that time. Then my mother added, "Hitler is not friendly to the Jews, but we won't have to worry because Holland will remain neutral. Besides, the queen will protect us." But clouds were appearing on the horizon, with Hitler gaining more and more power.

And so we took a Jewish couple into our home. As we listened to their plight and to the frightening accounts of what was going on in Germany, we found it difficult to imagine such destruction of Jewish lives and property. In school I had learned what a cultured and refined country Germany was, home to so many intellectuals. Now the seemingly impossible was happening.

✦━━✦

I was not too fond of the German couple staying with us. They seemed to upset the serenity of our home. The husband was demanding and forceful; I was used to my mother's gentleness. However, my sports activities and schooling compensated for the tension at home. I was an avid tennis player and spent most Sunday mornings on the tennis courts.

One day a handsome young man approached me and asked if I would play a doubles set with him and two of his friends. Flattered, I immediately said yes. I was impressed with this tall, interesting man with the strange accent who paid a lot of attention to me. He introduced himself as Felix. After the tennis match we went to the clubhouse to enjoy a friendly chat. I learned that Felix was from Germany and, with one of his brothers, had come to Holland several years before. The next week I met Felix again for more games of tennis. Afterward he invited me for a walk.

The year was now 1937; I was sixteen and it was a beautiful summer day. We walked for a long time, engaged in animated conversation. At one point we stopped at a teahouse for some lemonade. Here he discussed politics with me. I was not too interested and found that I was somewhat unfamiliar with what was happening in other countries. This was difficult for Felix to understand.

After many Sundays of playing tennis, I invited Felix to our home. My mother and brother were as impressed with him as I was. Felix, who was twenty-five, had a deep understanding of history, and I found I was learning a lot from him. He told me his mother still lived in Germany at this time, but his sister was already living in Holland.

Felix introduced me to his friends, who also had fled Germany. Each one had a horror story to tell. As the year sped by, tensions in Germany grew steadily worse. In March 1938 German troops marched into Austria. After assassinating Chancellor Dollfuss, Hitler annexed Austria. All of the bad news at that time seemed to be coming to a climax. When Hitler invaded Sudetenland in 1938, a part of Czechoslovakia, Felix and his brother and sister became adamant about getting their mother out of Germany. They said it was time for her to leave.

As time went on I became quite attached to Felix. My family and I were in awe of his knowledge concerning world events. I began to develop a certain feeling of security whenever we were together. I told myself that I was not afraid. I tried to suppress my fear and nervousness, which seemed to grow with each new horror story that I heard about Hitler and his treatment of Jews.

One day as Felix and I were walking, I said to him, "As long as the queen is here, I am not afraid."

He gave me a sorrowful look, and with a frown on his face, he replied, "Let me tell you something. Don't think for a moment that

Hitler is afraid of your queen. Believe me when I say that things don't look good for the Jews in Europe."

Remembering the words of my mother, I said, "Holland will remain neutral. How can things ever change here?"

Felix turned to me with a sad smile. "You are too naive to understand the situation." He then kissed me softly on the lips. With that, we went on our way.

Now it was time to get Felix's mother out of Germany. Felix planned to travel to his picturesque village in the south of Germany, located in a beautiful valley surrounded by mountains and rivers, where his family had lived for generations. But because Hitler had declared all Jews stateless, Felix needed a new passport to enter Germany. He went to the German consulate in Amsterdam to apply for one, was declared stateless, and received the passport with a big J (Jew) stamped on it.

When he arrived at his village in Germany, he found his mother bewildered by the political circumstances. She wanted to stay in her home. Felix explained what was happening in Germany and finally convinced her to go with him and leave everything behind. She left with tears streaming down her face, forced to say good-bye to the village and the home that she loved so much and where she had raised her children.

The lives of the Jewish people in Holland had also become frantic and chaotic. Many Jews wanted to leave Holland, but where would they go? It was difficult to immigrate to America. One needed visas to go to another European country. Some people had the opportunity to go to England. Others thought of Switzerland, where they had deposited funds.

By now it was the fall of 1938. A young man named Grunspan, the son of Polish Jews, had killed the secretary of the German embassy in Paris, Ernest Von Rath, because Grunspan's parents had been deported. In revenge, many Germans took part in what was called Kristallnacht, or "the breaking of the glass night." Kristallnacht was fueled, of course, by Hitler. Synagogues as well as businesses and homes owned by Jews were destroyed, and thousands of Jewish people from both Germany and Austria were arrested and sent to concentration camps. My mother, my sister, and I were agonized with fear.

One evening soon after, Felix came to our home and said, "I am not staying in Holland." He and his brother had prominent positions with a family-owned import-export grain company that had a branch in Rotterdam, and the company would help him to leave Holland.

I asked him, "What about England and France? Why don't they stop Hitler?"

"These countries are not prepared for war yet," he replied. "Mr. Chamberlain is in contact with Hitler."

I tried to change my foreboding thoughts and forced myself to think of pleasant things. But the horror of it all would not go away— not in our part of the world and not in my mind.

One evening in May of 1939, when Felix came to visit my family, the expression on his face told us something important was about to take place.

+>==<+

Felix had received word from family who still lived in Germany that they had finally found a way to get out. They had obtained visas to go to Cuba, a country that had given German refugees permission to enter. Of course, large sums of money were exchanged for these permits at the Cuban embassy, but at that time people would give up anything to get out of Germany and save their lives. On the evening of May 13, 1939, the biggest ship of the German company HAPAC, the SS *St. Louis*, left Hamburg with about one thousand people on board. The *St. Louis* was destined for Cuba.

Among the people aboard were writers, scientists, doctors, professors, and other intellectuals. Felix's family eagerly anticipated leaving a country that would destroy synagogues, burn books, destroy Jewish homes, and throw innocent people into concentration camps. It was clearly a country gone insane. But their anticipation was tinged with much sorrow. Some people had to leave their parents or older members of their families behind. They had to say farewell to their homes, their possessions, and a country where they had lived their whole life.

As the *St. Louis* approached the harbor in Havana, word came to the ship that the authorities would not let it dock. People began to panic; some wanted to jump overboard. The tension grew unbearable. Finally the Cuban authorities ordered the ship to return to Germany within twenty-four hours. Panic, chaos, and dread ensued.

As the ship made its way back, the coast of Florida came into view. Passengers could already see the skyscrapers of Miami in the distance. In a state of desperation, the captain of the SS *St. Louis* communicated by telegram with authorities in the United States.

When the ship reached the coast of Florida, the passengers were full of hope and excitement, convinced that the United States would allow them to disembark. But after days of negotiating, the

United States refused to take the refugees in. There was no help for the *St. Louis*. The ship sailed back to Germany—a destination of death for all aboard.

Holland took in about two hundred of these people, among them, one of Felix's relatives. Belgium and France also took in some passengers, but the remainder of the passengers were sent back to Germany, where they later perished in the concentration camps. It was now June of 1939, and what should have been a serene summer began to take on apocalyptic dimensions.

I stopped reading the newspapers. I only looked at the headlines each day to know what was happening. The entire time I carried a flicker of hope that things would change. They did not. On September 1, 1939, Hitler invaded the western part of Poland after he had made a secret agreement with the Soviet Union that it would occupy the eastern part of Poland.

Now that Hitler, the self-proclaimed Führer, had broken his promise for peace and resorted to continued aggression, England and France declared war on Germany during the first week of September 1939. It was dreadful—neighboring countries at war with each other? Germany, the refined country I had admired through my studies at school, the malicious aggressor? To hide my fear, I still clung to the idea that Holland would stay out of the war—that we would, as my mother always said, "stay neutral."

Then one evening in late October of 1939, when Felix visited our home, he was serious and somber and asked to speak with my mother alone. My sister and I insisted on staying in the room with them. "I have come to tell you that I just received a telegram from my company's office in Buenos Aires," he began. "They have arranged a visa for me for South America." He continued, facing my mother, "You know by now that I am a serious, down-to-earth person. I have read *Mein Kampf,* and I can judge what the Nazi movement is all about. I will leave Holland in a few weeks. I'm booking on a Dutch neutral ship. The idea is to go to Chile and from there to Argentina, where the headquarters of my company are located. The name of the ship that will take me there is the SS *Simon Bolivar.*"

We listened intently and tried to take it all in, but it was difficult to comprehend all that was about to happen with our beloved friend Felix. My mother was about to speak, but Felix interrupted. "I want to point out that there is much danger ahead of us. I feel that it is totally possible for the Germans to invade Holland." I had not taken it seriously when in the past Felix told me he would leave Holland. But that evening I was shocked. He was really leaving. My family would lose our rock, which is what Felix had become.

I looked at my mother's face. It was full of sorrow. That night it was raining very hard. The clatter against the window, the gush of the wind, the quiet pounce of the cat jumping onto my mother's lap, the internal thumping of my heart—I was acutely aware of these sounds invading our silence. That horrible foreboding feeling, the same feeling I had the day Opa died, overwhelmed me once again.

Felix took my hand in his, which caused me to leave my sad pondering and pay full attention to what was happening. His next words stunned me—and left everyone in my family speechless. "I can take Flory with me, even if we are not married. I can save her life, and I promise you that I will take care of her. At least she will not fall into the hands of the Nazis."

No one spoke. No one could. What Felix was proposing would alter the course of my life. Finally, my sister broke the silence. "We will have to talk to the family first," she said.

Felix turned to face my mother and spoke directly to her. "I know it is a big responsibility on my part, but this is better than falling prey to the Nazis." My mother nodded. "But first," he continued, "I must know if Flory wants to come with me. She is the one we are talking about. I give you my word, I will take good care of her."

The silence became so unbearable that just to break it I coughed a bit. I felt so sorry for my mother; her face looked pale and haunted. Once again my sister said, "We have to discuss it with the family."

Felix turned to her and said, "Let's first make sure that Flory wants to come with me. Then I will talk to your family and explain what my plans are." With a stern face he continued, "But I must have an answer soon. The timing is urgent and the ship will sail in a few weeks."

I felt numb. It was hard to absorb the idea of leaving Holland, my darling mother, my beloved family, and the country that I loved so much. But when Felix embraced me, I suddenly blurted out, "I want to go with Felix." After Felix left, I could feel the emotions of the evening coming to a climax. I knew I had to stick with my decision.

The next day we had another meeting at our house. My brothers had traveled in from Amersfoort and Amsterdam. My uncle, who was also my guardian, was also present. After Felix discussed his plans, my oldest brother, Ies, said to no one in particular, "I hope you know what you are doing."

My brother Ben turned to Felix and said, "It is a good idea to leave if you can make it. Remember, there is a war going on."

My uncle made an attempt to speak and started to say, "Don't you see," but by then everyone had begun to talk at once.

Ben said, "If America comes in, the war might be over soon. Hitler must be stopped. Felix knows what he is doing."

"Yes," I said. "I want to go with Felix."

We all kissed each other, cried, and hugged. The atmosphere was a mix of emotions: sadness, excitement, hope for the future. And so when Felix and the others had left, I went to my room to face a sleepless night. But the next morning I focused my thoughts on the future, and I put my trust in Felix.

CHAPTER 3

The Odyssey
of the SS *Simon Bolivar*

SS *Simon Bolivar*

Within a few days Felix had booked two cabins on the SS *Simon Bolivar*, an 8,300-ton passenger ship of the Royal Dutch Shipping Company. Destined for Curaçao (Netherlands Antilles), the ship would sail on Friday night, November 17, 1939, from Ijmuiden. From there it would go to Chile.

At home we said our tearful good-byes to our families—to my mother, sister and brothers, and Felix's family. At the railway station in Rotterdam, many friends and other relatives came to see us off. A prayer for our well-being was recited, and my mother and Felix's mother gave us their blessings. After all this, the emotions became too difficult for us to bear, and we finally boarded the train.

I could not look back anymore at my mother's dear, sweet face. The train slowly pulled away from the station, and we were on our way. I was eighteen years old.

On the way to Amsterdam, we did not speak much because both Felix and I were in a daze. We held hands. Felix said again, "I will take good care of you. All will be well, you'll see."

After we got off the train in Amsterdam, we continued to Ijmuiden, where the SS *Simon Bolivar* was situated in all her glory. Departure was that same night. I was glad; I wanted the time to go by quickly.

We inspected our cabins, checked our luggage, and walked around the ship a bit. There were four hundred people on board, including the crew. I saw on the passenger list that I was to share my cabin with an English girl. She was a charming girl who was on her way to Paramaribo, where she worked for an oil company as a secretary. Since I was fluent in English, we chatted amicably until late in the night. I woke up the next morning to a gloomy day. It was Saturday, November 18, 1939. I looked through the porthole of my cabin and noticed dense fog and ominous waters. My roommate was still sleeping soundly.

I was hungry, so I showered, dressed warmly, and left the cabin for breakfast. I met Felix near the staircase on deck. We noticed a lot of children on board, and people were chatting away in different languages: English, Dutch, German. We met other passengers who were also relieved to be able to leave Europe. The morning went by quickly, and after a while a band began to play music to entertain the passengers. As I listened to the music, I became restless and told Felix that I wanted to go on deck.

Standing on the deck, we looked out over the North Sea and sadly thought of our loved ones we had left behind. Soon more people joined us, and we became engaged in pleasant conversations—a distraction from our sad thoughts.

As the weather turned colder, I said to Felix, "I'm going to the cabin to get a scarf." On my way, I noticed that a clock on the staircase read 11:20 a.m. I chose a warm shawl out of my suitcase and wrapped it around my neck, over my coat.

When I returned to the deck, Felix and a few of the other passengers were involved in a lively conversation about politics. By that time it must have been about 11:45 a.m. Looking out over the water, I noticed something that looked like a tube or a pipe sticking out of the water. I turned to Felix and asked, "How does the captain know the way through all that—"

Before I could finish my sentence there was an enormous explosion. Felix was thrown against the floor of the deck with such force that he could not get up. I also hit the deck so hard that I could not move. Children were screaming, water was gushing all over, and people were yelling and moaning. Someone from the crew yelled, "Up, up! We have to get up!" Shattered glass lay everywhere. It was an apocalypse, a Dante's hell.

I turned to see that the young man who had been standing next to me was dead. The grand piano had fallen onto him and several other people. Felix and I could see each other in the midst of the bodies and the turmoil, but we could not communicate. There was blood all over.

Eventually—although I cannot remember how—I managed to crawl over to Felix. Somehow I half-carried, half-dragged him up the stairs to the highest point of the ship. There people were screaming, "The captain is dead!" "Where are the lifeboats?" "Where are my children?" "Where is my wife?" "Send out an SOS." We had never rehearsed safety procedures. During the explosion a large piece of glass had hit me in the neck. Blood was everywhere, and it became difficult to hold Felix up; he could not manage to stand on his own.

Within fifteen minutes there was another, even more violent, explosion. This time something must have hit the boiler room of the ship because oil was spouting everywhere. All of us had oil on our hair, faces, and bodies. I saw people running everywhere—people in their pajamas, people half dressed. There was even a woman naked running for her life. Some were clinging to their little babies; some jumped into the water. By now the ship was sinking fast. People panicked; there was screaming and chaos everywhere.

When we reached the water, the waves hit us with extreme force. Swimming was out of the question because of the thick layer of oil. Felix and I managed to hang onto a heavy rope. I remember going underwater.

In retrospect, I believe it was sheer force of will, the rush of adrenaline, and the power of the spirit to stay alive that helped us to hang onto the rope that tragic day. With so many bones broken in our bodies, it should have been impossible for us to cling so tightly.

Shortly after the second explosion, a crew member threw big pieces of wood into the water, and several other crew members tried to get some of the lifeboats lowered. It was futile because the second explosion caused many of the lifeboats to disappear along with the people in them.

We clung to the wood and the rope, and I kept going underwater because I was wearing a heavy coat. Felix kept yelling to me to hang on and not to let go. I was in shock, not believing it was real. Finally, we were drawn into a lifeboat that was half filled with water. It was difficult for us to think or collect our thoughts. A man began to pray loudly. Another man was lying against my legs, blood spurting from his head. He was either dead or unconscious.

Our ship, the majestic SS *Simon Bolivar,* had sunk in a matter of minutes after the second explosion. I looked back from the lifeboat, but there was nothing to see of the ship except for the masts. All I saw were drowning people—death and destruction in a thick shroud of black machine oil.

At that moment I believed that our ship had been torpedoed. Later we learned that two German mines had caused this terrifying tragedy. Those magnetic mines had been placed there the night before by the German U-boats *Bernd von Arnim, Wilhelm Heidkamp,* and *Hermann Kuenne.*

Our "lifeboat" was quickly filling with water. The sea was so wild that the waters caused it to jerk back and forth, up and down; several times the boat tilted into a vertical position with all of us hanging on. The wounded man against my legs had rolled over; I was sure he was dead.

I saw that Felix was lying between two other people in the lifeboat. His face was unrecognizable and distorted from pain. I thought to myself, "This is the end. I hope the drowning goes fast."

The nightmare, though, continued. Everyone was praying as loudly as they could. A tall man in the boat said, midway through his prayers, "The captain is dead. He was killed immediately." We were quickly losing hope; there seemed to be no way out of this ordeal.

Darkness began to set in. The fog grew even more dense. It seemed as if hours and hours had gone by. What if no one rescued us? I prayed, "Please, God, let it be fast. Let it be over quickly."

Suddenly, someone yelled, "A ship, I see a ship!" No one reacted at first, thinking it had been a mirage. But a ship was certainly approaching; we could see its outline in the midst of the fog.

The ship came closer and closer as the tall man in our boat screamed, "It's a British destroyer! We will be saved!" Indeed, it was a British ship. Those on board had heard on their radio that the SS *Simon Bolivar* had been destroyed during an explosion. The ship had spotted us.

After much maneuvering, the destroyer was able to come close to our lifeboat. The British sailors then had the impossible task of getting us on board their ship. They could not approach us too closely for fear they would smash our small lifeboat to pieces. First they threw out lines, but the high waves and dense fog obstructed their rescue attempts. The crew yelled something to us, but their voices were devoured by the roar of the sea. It was November, very cold, and the rescue seemed like an impossible task. We were beyond help, I thought, hanging on in our wet clothes, drenched in oil, and physically wounded. But praise be to the courageous British sailors—they did not give up on their lifesaving mission.

They persisted, and eventually they lowered cranes into the sea. One by one, the victims were placed in a net, first me and then the men. After our rescue I did not see Felix again until much later. I eventually learned that the British sailors, after rescuing Felix and safely positioning him on deck, transported him to the Royal Naval Hospital in Ipswich.

After I was hoisted up I was placed in a small cabin. A nun, who apparently had also been on the SS *Simon Bolivar*, removed my clothes and dressed me in something belonging to the crew. I lay down and a female crew member gave me something hot to drink. The next few hours were a blur to me. Eventually I realized I was on a stretcher. Was the ordeal really over? It sank in: I had been rescued. But where was Felix? Was he all right? I also began to think of how the family members of the passengers of the SS *Simon Bolivar* would react once they heard the news of the ship's demise.

We would later learn that 104 people had lost their lives, their hopes and dreams disappeared forever in the depths of the North Sea.

As I lay in the stretcher worrying about Felix, an air raid warning began to sound. People ran away in every direction, but one sailor remained by my side. At that moment I did not care if I was dead or alive. I heard airplanes flying overhead, and I asked the sailor where I was.

He replied, "You are on the ship docked in Harwich; you are safe now. I'll stay here with you."

I said to him, "Could you please send a telegram to my family?"

He said he would. Frustrated and confused, I could not remember my mother's name or the names of my other family members or the friends who had accompanied us to the train station upon our departure.

I told the sailor that I could not remember anything. He calmed me down, and after the sound of the sirens abated, the name NIDERA, the company where Felix had worked, popped into my head. I requested the sailor to send the telegram to NIDERA in Rotterdam.

Later I found out that, indeed, our families received the wire informing them that we both had been saved from the demise of the SS *Simon Bolivar*.

+⊨══⊨+

I was dazed and found myself in a hospital bed. After removing glass from my forehead, they examined my neck again. They called another doctor into the examining room, and they all began to work on my neck. Suddenly I heard a thud. An object was thrown into a container near where I lay. It was a large piece of glass from the ship's porthole, which had become lodged in my neck after the explosion. It was probably the only thing that was left of the SS *Simon Bolivar*. I still have this piece of glass, and keep it in my purse. The two doctors and the nurses were in awe—it was a miracle. The large piece of glass had been lodged just a millimeter away from my carotid artery.

The next day my wrist and hand were operated on. The doctors put me in a cast from my hand to my elbow. Two days later the nurses attended to my hair, which was a bunch of clustered strings saturated in oil. I had very long hair, and for a long time the nurses were discussing what to do with it. They must have tried a number of chemicals on my hair because when they were done, I was blond with short hair. I did not recognize myself.

Several days went by, and during the quiet moments I wondered what my fate would be. I hoped that the friendly sailor who had stayed by my side on the ship had sent the telegram to Rotterdam and that my family knew we had been saved.

It was the third day after I was brought to the hospital that the Dutch consul came to visit me at my bedside. He was accompanied by a friendly gentleman by the name of Mr. Bland. They asked me all kinds of questions because, of course, I had no papers, and all we had taken with us on the SS *Simon Bolivar* lay now at the bottom of the sea. I told them that I had been on board with my friend Felix, and I relayed as much information as I could, hoping they could bring us together. The English authorities had a tremendous task figuring out who belonged to whom. All the while air raid sirens were going on and off.

Shortly after this, much to my relief and delight, Felix's brother came to the hospital where I was. He had flown over to England from Holland to determine what kind of state we were in. I was so happy to see a familiar face. He promised to find Felix and see to it that we were cared for in the same hospital. We were among the most seriously injured survivors of the ship's explosions. We did not know it then, but we were to remain hospitalized for over six months.

In the meantime, journalists came to see me, filming and interviewing me. I was featured in the news in Holland and learned later that my family saw me lying in the hospital bed.

Within a few more days, the Dutch consul came again and told me that he had located the hospital in Ipswich where Felix was, and soon I would be transferred there.

Mr. Bland, the gentleman who had accompanied the consul during the initial visit, drove me to Ipswich. He promised to take great care of me. At the time, being in pain and under much duress, I simply accepted the generosity of this stranger. It was much later that I realized the true heart and soul of this wonderful man. He was socially prominent and president of Barclay's Bank, one of the largest banks in England. He was deeply concerned about the atrocities caused by Hitler and the war and the pain and suffering of others. Mr. Bland became my guardian angel; I was fortunate to have come under his care.

Finally, finally, I was reunited with my friend Felix. Unfortunately, I found him in terrible shape. A few days later Mr. Bland introduced me to the head of the hospital, who explained in some detail Felix's condition.

I was led to an office where I met Felix's doctor. Mr. Bland advised me to address him as "mister" and not "doctor" for in England "mister" connotes greater prestige.

First, the doctor reiterated the terrible ordeal Felix and I had been through and expressed his concern. He then told me about Felix's injuries. Felix had broken his pelvis and damaged his urinary tract, which caused terrible pain and made it impossible for him to urinate normally. We had a long conversation, and the doctor even drew some diagrams for me so I would better understand Felix's injuries.

However, I did not understand the seriousness of Felix's condition until the doctor said, frowning, "I must let you know that your friend is so seriously wounded that there is a great possibility he will never walk again." I began to cry, and both men patted me on the back. The doctor said in a consoling tone, "It is best that you do not tell Felix this. I can assure you that we here in Ipswich will do our utmost to get him well." And with that I went back to Felix's ward. I did not reveal to him the devastating news I had just heard.

It was now the end of November, and the weather was bitter cold. Felix and I were under the care of a special nurse whose compassion was enormous. She went out of her way to make us comfortable. In time she became like a second mother to me; I grew to love her dearly. I was still in my teens and in need of a lot of reassurance. Her name was Sister Jeannie, and I have never forgotten her.

Of the two of us, Felix suffered more. He was placed flat on his back in bed with two heavy sandbags on either side of his body to keep him from moving. But my injuries caused me much pain and inconvenience, and eventually I felt that I could not stand it any longer. Mr. Bland, who visited us every day, noticed my agony. One day he took me aside in the hospital lobby and said in a serious tone, "I'm going to take you to the best physician, a bone specialist. I know he can help you."

The next day he made an appointment for me with this specialist, who gave me a complete physical examination. His staff took lots of X-rays, examined me for a long time, and discovered that I had multiple fractures of my ribs, knee, and wrist that had not been set properly. Because of the heavy explosions, I was thrown onto the deck of the SS *Simon Bolivar* so furiously that I had suffered multiple fractures on the left side of my body. My knee had also been injured during the explosion at sea. The next day I was put in a body cast. I was not required to remain immobile in bed, but the cast caused me great difficulty in walking. I had to hobble. Because there were so many seriously injured military people in the hospital, the medical staff needed all of the beds available. Besides, I was young and had amazing willpower and was determined to get around by myself.

Mr. Jones, the bone specialist, advised me to undergo another operation on my wrist. But I was so fearful of the crude anesthetic that I adamantly refused. "You are a silly girl," he said, and he was right; I have been sorry all my life that I did not heed his advice. Not only would my wrist look deformed to me later in my life, but playing the piano with that hand was extremely difficult.

But now there was the issue of where I would go next. My guardian angel, Mr. Bland, told me that Felix would have to remain in the hospital for a long time. "So why don't I see to it," he said, "that you are set up in a boarding home where you can comfortably recuperate?" I liked the idea, and within a few days he came to the hospital to tell me that he had found the perfect place.

The boardinghouse was owned and operated by a Miss Morling, a sweet, kind, elderly woman. Mr. Bland made it clear to her how important it was to take good care of me. The fact that he was president of Barclay's Bank must have impressed Miss Morling because I felt as if the red carpet was rolled out for me. The house was a typical English country home surrounded by many large trees and lush bushes. At that time of the year there were no flowers in bloom, but one could imagine, even during the cold winter, how lovely the grounds would look in spring and summer.

Miss Morling's guests were all young people. I had to share my bedroom with another girl whose name was Emma. She was very beautiful with flaming red hair. She was also sweet, kind, and helpful to me. She reminded me of my roommate on the SS *Simon Bolivar* with whom I had shared a cabin for only one night, whose hopes and dreams were now at the bottom of the sea. Each time I thought of her, tears came to my eyes.

There was only one open fireplace in the house located in the living room. I had to share the bed with Emma, but we didn't mind because the temperature was so cold at night. Emma had to get up very early in the morning to go to work. We each had a jar with water to wash ourselves; we always washed very quickly and then went to the open fireplace to warm ourselves. I hobbled along with Emma, who helped me down the stairs. Mr. Bland came to visit me each morning promptly at 8:30; I could have set my clock by his visits. He was very concerned about my well-being.

Miss Morling had a cheerful manner that was contagious. For some reason she nicknamed me Dolly and called me her "little Dutch Dolly." One morning, many days after I had arrived at her boardinghouse, she said to me, "How would you like to go for a walk?" I was eager to get out, and I enthusiastically accepted her invitation. She continued, "We can walk to the hospital. You will see that it is not far." And so we went, Miss Morling walking beside me as I hobbled along in my body cast.

When we arrived at the hospital, we went through the long corridors to get to Felix's room. Poor Felix was in constant pain. There was nothing we could do for him; we were all helpless. At that time we did not have the medical research and technology we have today. But we did have Nurse Jeannie, who did her best to cheer us up. While we were visiting Felix that day, Nurse Jeannie said to me, "Do you know there are Dutch sailors from the SS *Simon Bolivar* in the next ward?" She led us through another corridor. What a surprise! Four or five Dutch people from the crew of the ship were lying there. We all began to talk at once. They too had suffered multiple fractures but were not as badly hurt as Felix.

I enjoyed talking with them. The Dutch are accustomed to eating a lot, and they asked us if we had access to food stores. Of course we said we would try to get them what they wanted and be back the next day. On the way back to the boardinghouse, I apologized to Miss Morling for talking for so long in my native language to the sailors. She said she did not mind, so I recounted the entire conversation to her in English.

As young and naive as I was, the next day I decided I could go to the hospital on my own. Miss Morling was very reluctant, so I said to her, "Ask Mr. Bland's opinion." The next day she did, but Mr. Bland frowned and told me quite firmly that he felt I should wait a few more days. With all the air raids, I needed to know my way around much better than I did.

Though there were strict visiting hours at the hospital, Nurse Jeannie allowed me to visit anytime because she knew how much I wanted to be with Felix. I never divulged a word to him about what his doctor discussed with me, but I continued to worry about his progress. I later discussed the matter with Mr. Bland. He looked pensive and said, "I've spoken with Felix's physician. His injuries are very serious and might take a long time to heal." I felt a slight panic set in until Mr. Bland reassured me. "Be patient," he continued. "I promise that we here in England will take good care of both of you. You'll have the best care possible. Don't worry. It will be all right." With that, he left me in the good care of Miss Morling.

By now it was the end of December; we had been in England for over a month. Christmas and New Year's were approaching. I had become more or less accustomed to my life with darling Miss Morling hovering over me and Mr. Bland supervising. Some of the boarders had gone home for the Christmas season, among them my roommate, Emma. I missed her very much. She helped me climb the stairs every night, which was a difficult task for me with my cast. Besides, it was pleasant to talk with her before going to sleep.

From time to time, Mr. Bland took me to his country home. It was a beautiful, large estate located on acres of exquisitely landscaped property—something out of a British movie. The facade of the house took my breath away when I saw it for the first time.

Mrs. Bland was a charming woman. She, her husband, and family welcomed me graciously on my first visit. The inside of their home was as tasteful as the outside—in particular, their library. The walls were adorned with beautifully framed paintings that had been in the family for centuries. There were paintings of their ancestors as well as masterpieces acquired from famous artists.

Back at the boardinghouse, Miss Morling was getting ready for Christmas. She took me with her to buy a modest Christmas tree, which I helped her trim and decorate. Walking was still awkward for me, and the cast felt very cold on my body. Despite this, I was swept away in the gaiety of it all and in the atmosphere Miss Morling created. I was thinking that at this time of year it was also Hanukkah, the Festival of Lights and the Festival of Freedom and Dedication. I was sure that no one in Ipswich knew what Hanukkah was. As the saying goes, "When in Rome, do as the Romans." So I joined in the celebration of Christmas, mostly because I genuinely loved Miss Morling. We felt very comfortable in each other's company in spite of our different religions.

Just before Christmas I received an unexpected surprise. Early one morning the doorbell rang. When Miss Morling opened the door, a gentleman in a naval officer's uniform stood there. He identified himself as a crew member of the destroyer that had rescued survivors of the SS *Simon Bolivar*. He had found out that I was living in the boardinghouse, and he asked Miss Morling if he could say hello to me. She hesitated at first, but he seemed honest so she let him in and called me.

When I came into the living room, I was thrilled to see the officer who had stood by me on the ship docked in Harwich when the air raid sirens went off and everyone else went running. We hugged, and I cried and thanked him over and over again. He told me that he had in fact sent the telegram of our rescue to Rotterdam, as I had asked him to do. When I asked him his name, he identified himself only as "James." He explained that he could not divulge the name of the destroyer or where he came from. After all, a war was going on; secrets had to be kept. But on that morning we rejoiced. I told him all about Felix. Unfortunately, our visit was short. After he left I never saw or heard from him again.

That afternoon I went to the hospital and told Felix about my surprise. He was still in much pain, and I stayed with him a long time, unaware that evening had come and darkness had set in. When I said good-bye to Felix, I quickly went to the Dutch sailors' ward to say hello. When I left the hospital, I saw that fog had set in. As I walked away, an air raid siren suddenly went off, which meant that I had to stay where I was. It was quite a while before I could continue homeward, but now I had lost my way. It was terrifying.

Everything was pitch-dark. I went first in one direction, then another, up and down different streets, until I realized I was truly lost. Panic set in until I finally ran into someone to whom I explained my predicament. Luckily, he was a constable and immediately escorted me to the boardinghouse. By this time it was quite late, and Miss Morling had already sent her young men out to find me.

Both of us, Felix and I, must have had a guardian angel watching over us.

┼══❯══❮┼

Christmas and New Year's came and went. The first two months of 1940 went by rather uneventfully. Again I visited my doctor, Mr. Jones, who told me that soon my cast would come off. As far as Felix was concerned, they would try to get him out of bed in a few weeks. In the meantime, Theo, Felix's brother, visited us again. He advised us to try to stay in England. Of course Felix, in the condition he was in, could hardly move, let alone leave England.

Finally at the end of February, my cast came off. It felt very strange at first, and I was dizzy. Mr. Jones again strongly recommended resetting my wrist to correct the problem, but I did not feel like having another operation. He warned me that my wrist would never be the same.

The month of March approached, and one afternoon Nurse Jeannie told me that the hospital staff would try to get Felix out of bed the next morning when Mr. Jones would be there. I arrived at the hospital very early the next morning. When Mr. Jones came into Felix's room, the anticipation was palpable. I know it was quite a painful ordeal for Felix, but he was able to stand on his own feet for a few moments. And what a moment that was for all of us!

Mr. Jones came to see Felix every day. He ordered a therapist who could help Felix perform exercises to strengthen his body so he could walk again. We all held our breath for many, many days. It was the love and encouragement of all of the nurses and doctors that finally, finally, at the beginning of April 1940, got Felix to slowly walk down the hospital corridors on his own.

Of course we had to be patient, but now Felix and I could at least contemplate the next steps we would take toward our future. We had been in England for five and one-half months, in and out of hospitals. All I could think of was going back to my mother, but Felix thought it wiser to remain in England until we could try again to go to South America.

Around the second week of April Miss Morling came to my room waving a newspaper. She looked distressed as she said to me, "Dolly, Hitler has invaded Denmark and Norway. France and England are sending troops.... Oh, my goodness," she lamented, "where will all of this lead to?" Shortly after, all the young men in the boardinghouse had to report for military duty overseas.

By the end of April Felix could walk well enough so that he was able to do a few things for himself. Mr. Bland suggested that Felix stay at Miss Morling's boardinghouse so he could fully recuperate. I remember the day Felix arrived at Miss Morling's. In spite of his physical limitations at the time, Felix resorted to his old active self. He wasted no time trying to get in touch with the authorities to obtain a permit to stay in England. But this was not to be. Felix was a native of Germany, and that was enough reason for the British to refuse him a permanent stay. Even though Felix was at the boardinghouse, he was still under the doctor's care every day. I was glad that I had never told Felix about the doctor's original prognosis that he might not walk again.

Now the time had come for Felix and me to start talking about arrangements to return to Holland. In the shipwreck we had lost all of our possessions, and we had no insurance. The shipping company, the Royal Dutch Shipping Company, had, of course, paid for our stay and our medical care in England. Now they had to plan our return. We now knew that Denmark and Norway had been invaded by Hitler at the beginning of April. Traveling by ship was too dangerous; thus arrangements were made for us to return to Holland by airplane.

One morning Miss Morling came to me crying. She said to me, as best as she could through her tears, "You know, Dolly, I will never forget you. I will pray for you and Felix, for your safe return to Holland, and for your well-being, always. I hate to see you go." I also started to cry. This small, gray-haired woman had nursed me, suffered with me, helped me to keep my spirits up during one of the most trying times of my life, and watched over me all these months. We clung to each other. In her hand she clutched the little red book that contained the music I had played on the organ each week. "I want you to have my hymnal book as a memento," she said. "Look inside. I have inscribed it."

I took the book from her and read the following poem that she had written on the first page of *Alexander's Hymns No. 3:*

I know not what awaits me,
God kindly veils mine eyes;
And over each step of my onward way

He makes such scenes to rise.
And with every joy He sends me,
comes a sweet and glad surprise.

To my little Dutch Dolly, with heaps of love,
Ethel Morling
Ipswich, April 1940

We also said a tearful good-bye to Mr. and Mrs. Bland, thanking them profoundly for their care, hospitality, love, and encouragement during these trying months.

We left Ipswich early in the morning of May 1, 1940, for London, where we would board the airplane back to Holland. The next morning, May 2 (Felix's birthday), someone from the Dutch consulate came to take us to the airport in London. When we reached the airport, the plane that would take us home had *Holland* painted in large letters across it. I was so overcome with emotion that I almost fainted. However, that old foreboding feeling, almost like an omen, once again hit me, and I said, "I'm not going."

Felix became upset, and the person from the Dutch consulate who had driven us to the airport said to me, "There is no other way but to step in."

I had to go. The flight, albeit a short one, was awful and frightening for me. The plane, of course, was small, and the windows were blacked out. There were only a few people on board. I heard planes flying around us, and someone remarked that he hoped they were not German planes. They probably were.

At last we landed safely in Amsterdam, where I fell into the arms of my mother and my other family members. My sister held a large bouquet of flowers for us. Lots of people were waiting at home for us to welcome us back. On that day the festivities in honor of our return well made up for the suffering we had endured over the past six months. I was home with my darling mother. And so the first part of our journey through the Valley of Death was over.

CHAPTER 4

Holland Invaded

With Felix before returning to Holland from England

The first two days after we arrived home from England were
lively. A constant stream of family and friends visited our home,
bringing food, presents, and clothing for us. They wanted to know
every detail about the shipwreck, our recovery, and our six-month
stay in England.

My mother did not look well. I found that she had aged; of course,
she worried incessantly about us. Now that I was home, I hoped that
she would feel better. The Saturday following our return, my mother
suggested that we all go to synagogue to say prayers of thanks for our
safe return. There were quite a number of worshippers that day. The
rabbi said a special prayer of thanks, and the cantor sang special

psalms of grace befitting the occasion. I also became closer to Felix's family as a result of all we had been through together.

Several days after our return Felix told me that he was not giving up on his plans to leave Holland and that he had booked the two of us on the SS *Van Rensselaer*, a passenger liner also owned by the Royal Dutch Shipping Company. The ship would sail on May 11, 1940. I did not dare mention this to our families, but Felix's brother Theo was aware of our plans. Theo was a rock of support to both of us.

Felix and I needed new papers, passports, proof of this, proof of that, and it took much time to travel on the bus or the tram to go to the different agencies to acquire the needed paperwork.

The days went by very quickly, and we continued to get a lot of attention from people around us. I wrote to our friends in England to let them know we had arrived safely. But in the midst of our reunions and celebrations, there was no real peace. On the radio we heard that German planes were constantly flying over Holland.

Just as my family made plans to visit my brother in Amersfoort for a short vacation, again terror struck. It was May 10, 1940. I was awakened at about four o'clock in the morning by the sound of loud noises and low-flying planes. At first I thought I was dreaming, but then my mother rushed into my room looking white as a sheet. In a stammering voice she said, "Get up and get dressed! It must be the Germans."

The impossible was happening—war in Holland. Our flat was located near a railroad station, one of the first targets of the Germans. We heard bombs exploding all over the city. Neighbors on our street were running in different directions, shouting and gesturing wildly and appearing not to know what to do next. Not only were we in fear for our lives, but the concept of war in Holland was heartrending. Holland was a peace-loving country and had not experienced war in two hundred years.

At seven o'clock in the morning, my mother's sister and her youngest son, Jacob (my favorite cousin), came to our door. They both looked weary, frightened, and bewildered. "I want you all to come home with us," my aunt said. The radio was on, and we heard the announcer say that Germany was invading Holland.

My aunt told us that she and her sons would not want to live in a country occupied by Nazis; there was something ominous in the way she spoke. We felt the same. After a short while my aunt went home, leaving us with our thoughts, not knowing what to do next.

Finally my sister said, "I'm going to Felix's home." My mother still seemed undecided about what to do. I realized that it was difficult for her to leave everything behind. After my sister left, my mother and I gathered up our most important papers and valuable items and set out for Felix's home also. His family lived in Blijdorp, which was a suburb of Rotterdam.

Under normal circumstances it was a mere twenty-minute walk from our home to Felix's. On this day it took us several hours. We were worried about my sister. The bombings in our city were relentless, and we had to stop and hide each time we heard a bomb. Several times Dutch soldiers who appeared quite nervous stopped us and asked for papers, for our nationality, where we were going, who we were. This seemed so absurd to me. We had never needed any identification papers in Holland before. But now there was a war going on in my beloved country, and all had changed overnight.

As our long trip to Felix's home progressed, my mother began to pale again, and I was afraid that something might happen to her. Finally, after what seemed an eternity, we arrived to find Felix's mother, his brother Theo, sister Nellie, and, of course, my sister, Bep (our nickname for Elisabeth). But Felix was not there.

With much anxiety Theo explained that Felix, on his way to our home, had been stopped by Dutch soldiers who had interrogated him about his citizenship. At that time Felix wore a mustache and an English raincoat, which made him look typically German. Now the Dutch soldiers had received orders to intern all foreign subjects.

Felix's family had somehow received word that Felix, along with many other aliens, had been interned in De Doelen, a large concert hall in the center of Rotterdam. Upon seeing our worried faces, Theo explained in a sorrowful voice that the Dutch police were taking all aliens to their headquarters, to which they were required to report. All of us were very upset yet continued to expect Felix to walk through the door at any moment. I thought to myself, Did we go through that six-month ordeal, which is finally behind us, only to be separated or killed? Felix's mother was fervently Orthodox and always had her prayer book with her. She went into another room in the house, and we all knew she was praying very hard for her son.

A few days went by. We were in agony. We could see Rotterdam burning and could even smell the smoke. Still no Felix. We heard on the radio that The Hague had been hit, that the Germans had ruined a great deal of the west coast, and that thousands of people in Rotterdam had lost their lives. We also heard that Belgium and Luxembourg as well as France had all been attacked on that tragic day of May 10, 1940. Belgium, Luxembourg, and the Netherlands surrendered after five days of relentless bombing and destruction. France held out against the Germans for about three weeks but capitulated beginning in June 1940. In our minds it was already the end of the world.

Three days went by, four days, and still no sign of Felix. Looking at Felix's mother, I could tell that she was desperate, but outwardly she tried to appear calm. On the fifth day of the bombing the radio announcer told listeners that the Dutch had capitulated and the queen and her children had fled the country. This announcement threw me into emotional shock. Both events— Felix lost somewhere, and our queen fleeing—had a devastating effect on my nerves. It was a deep feeling of abandonment. Felix's words came back to me, words I had not believed: "I assure you that Hitler is not afraid of your queen." I had hoped that they were just rumors.

Finally, after what seemed like an eternity of bombing, burning, killing, and merciless destruction of the city of Rotterdam, the German troops marched in. The city was a sea of fire. But that did not deter the Germans. Stepping over the dead and wounded, they marched on singing "Gloria Victoria." This was the proud, so-called master race that the Dutch had to put up with for many years to come.

The German soldiers also marched into Blijdorp and onto our street. We had been sitting on the stairs for the past five days to protect ourselves from the bombing. Suddenly there was a sharp knocking at the door. Panic ensued; it was a German soldier. We didn't know what to do.

The knocking continued. My sister got up, kissed and hugged everyone, and said, crying bitterly, "Until I see you all in the hereafter."

Finally, Nellie went to the door and opened it a crack. The German soldier told her that the troops needed pots, pans, utensils, and other items. We could hear her speaking in German to the soldier, and she gave him what he asked for. Then we saw more soldiers going to neighbors on the street and loading up on different items from their homes.

Some hours later Theo said to us, "I'm going to find out what happened to Felix." Felix's mother turned white but did not hold him back. A long time went by, and the house was full of tension. Finally, after many hours, another miracle occurred: both Theo and Felix walked through the door. In an unbelievable set of circumstances, Theo found Felix wandering about the city. Felix looked terrible. He was unshaven, unwashed, quite thin, and his coat was almost in rags. But, thank goodness, we had him back with us. As we hovered around him, he told us what had happened to him over the past several days.

The bombs had destroyed the concert hall where he and other foreigners had been interned. After the guard fled, he and several others fled also. On his way back home several Dutch soldiers accosted him and took him to the cellar of a home, where he was locked up with other men who turned out to be escapees from the local jail.

At this point Felix was still in the hands of the Dutch. After the capitulation, the Germans took over all homes where they heard people in the cellar. Felix told the other men to be still. He yelled in German that German people were locked up here. A German officer opened the cellar door and detained all of them. Felix and the others had to walk for hours with the German troops through De Maasbrug, located in the southern part of the city where everything was burning. It looked like a place of slaughter.

The Germans then seized what had been a school, detained the men in the building, and announced that all men would be deported to Germany. Felix approached a high-ranking officer and told him that he was German and did not belong in this place. The first officer did not respond to him, and neither did the second. Finally, toward morning, a third officer listened to him and let him go.

Was it a guardian angel again who watched over him and protected him? All of us said prayers of thanks, and Felix's mother prepared and served a good meal. Afterward, Felix cleaned up, and soon friends and neighbors stopped by. The conversation went on late into the evening.

We were still alive, all of us together, and the next step was to find out where my aunt, uncle, and cousins were and how our friends had fared during that terrible week. Here again, God had been with us, and though we did not know what the future would bring, we could extract some hope that again we would survive.

My mother, sister, and I stayed on for a few days at the home of Felix and his family. But eventually my mother said, "We cannot stay here forever. We must go home and see what has happened."

I cannot describe the complete chaos we discovered on our way home; we realized it had been a miracle that we were not killed by the bombs. From what we saw on the streets, entire neighborhoods were completely destroyed. German soldiers were everywhere. We saw Dutch soldiers being led at gunpoint by the Germans to be deported. Dead bodies lay all over the streets where they had fallen.

Although the railroad station had been badly damaged, we found our flat in the same condition as we had left it. With a very serious, almost despondent look on her face, my mother said to my sister and me, "We know what it will be like for Jewish people under a German regime; we must get some valuables together and bring them to the neighbors." She immediately began to gather photographs—from our youth, from our school days, of our grandparents, and of other family members.

The next day we packed up three large suitcases, just in case. At least we still had each other. We had word that my brother and his wife in Amersfoort were fine, but we had no word of my brother Ben, in Amsterdam.

The day we packed our suitcases, my sister said, "We have not heard from Aunt Sien and the family; we must go there and find out how they are." My aunt lived not far from us, so later in the day the three of us walked to their home to find it was still standing. But where were they? Panic set in, and we were worried about their welfare. After making many telephone calls and talking to mutual friends, we learned the terrible news that my aunt, uncle, and their two sons had all tried to commit suicide, as did so many others who preferred death to torture when the Germans marched into the city. They had taken a lethal dose of morphine that they had obtained from a pharmacist friend. All became violently ill. My twenty-six-year-old cousin, Maurits, had died. Jacob, the younger brother, and my uncle, the brilliant chess master, survived the attempt. My poor aunt, however, suffered a stroke and was in a nearby hospital.

The oldest son, Simon, lived in Amsterdam and had escaped this ordeal. We wondered if things would have turned out differently had Simon been with his family. He had a way of dealing with difficult situations, and perhaps he would have talked them out of choosing to end their lives.

When we arrived at the hospital to see my aunt, we found her in a frightful condition. Her face and arms were covered with yellow spots that looked like burn marks. The nurse on duty explained that an assistant, in an attempt to revive my poor aunt, had put hot water bottles on her body, which turned out to be too hot. Because of the stroke my aunt was unable to communicate this to the assistant and ended up with burn marks all over her body. As gently as possible, we tried to explain to my aunt the fate of her son Maurits. We had the feeling that somehow she already knew. Maurits had been a handsome, most intelligent young man with a bright future ahead of him. My uncle was slowly recovering after his suicide attempt.

The next day the funeral of my cousin Maurits took place at a Jewish cemetery, Het Toepad, which was located east of Rotterdam.

My sister and I, as well as friends and neighbors, attended. The rabbi of Rotterdam conducted the somber event. Every word the rabbi spoke was like a pearl of wisdom. In a simple wooden coffin my cousin was laid to rest, and we all recited Kaddish, the prayer for departed loved ones, which confirms our faith in God and does not include complaints of our adversities. During this hour of grief, I could only think of the overwhelming confusion. I kept staring at the words on the gate at the entrance of the cemetery, which read, "He who is born must die; he who dies enters life eternal." I tried to contemplate these words and make sense of what was happening, but it did not help. After the funeral, we were both physically and emotionally exhausted, especially considering we had to bicycle both to and from the cemetery.

At home that night, we turned on the radio and learned, much to our consternation, that many prominent intellectuals in Holland had taken their lives as well. They knew what a Nazi regime would entail—concentration camps and persecutions. They too had chosen death over torture.

The weeks following the invasion were marked with the typical German characteristics of diplomatic double-talk. Right after the military settled in the SS followed, and the Dutch newspapers were subjected to censorship. Over the next several days we read bold headlines in the newspapers announcing that Hitler had appointed Dr. Arthur Seyss-Inquart as head of the German occupation forces in Holland. Seyss-Inquart was an Austrian lawyer, a fanatical Nazi, and a staunch follower of Hitler's orders who had betrayed his own country to Hitler.

In the short time that the Germans had been in our country, they already had seized many government buildings. It was bizarre to the Dutch when the newspapers announced that Seyss-Inquart was to present a speech in the famous Ridderzaal (Knight's Hall) in The Hague, the beautiful place where our queen always presented her yearly "Troonrede" (loosely translated, state of the union speech). This event was always celebrated with much joy and festivities in the month of September (Prinsjesdag). We did not feel this festive spirit in the anticipation of Seyss-Inquart's speech. He spoke about a master race, the Aryan race, *Arbeit macht frei* (work gives freedom), the victory of the Germans, and how Germany had won for Europe. He also vowed to get rid of the Jews. We turned the radio on and off, but it seemed as if this speech lasted forever. That night I found that I hated the German language; it seemed harsh and distasteful to me.

We had a number of German collaborators in Holland, called the Nationaal Socialistische Beweging, or the NSB. The most notorious of them was a man named Mussert, a civil engineer. The NSB helped the Germans to familiarize themselves with the customs and culture of my country. In addition to all of the atrocities was the humiliation that the Germans referred to our country as the Westland or the Western Province of Germany.

Soon the Nazis started to heap shameless insults on the Jews. For instance, they showed a film to both the Nazis and the members of the NSB called *Der Ewige Jude*, meaning "The Eternal Jew." The film depicted Jewish people as rats. This was only the beginning. These events had a most nerve-racking effect on the Jewish population. We began to panic.

My sister went back to live with the family for whom she worked in the countryside. We were grateful that my oldest brother, Ies, and his wife in Amersfoort were in satisfactory condition considering the circumstances. But we were extremely concerned about my brother Ben for we still had received no word. My mother became the strong one now; I leaned on her for strength and reassurance. She said to me, "You have to be strong; we will get through this somehow." She continued, "I have confidence in Ben; he knows what he is doing." We knew that Ben had many friends in Belgium and in England, but we could not begin to imagine what had happened to him.

Our neighbors and non-Jewish friends were marvelous. They visited our home often and would try to say comforting things, like, "Don't take things literally. Anti-Semitism is built into the German system." Or they would try to console us with the reassurance that "this is just Nazi politics; don't take it so hard."

Many Christian citizens protested heavily against the hatred the Germans invoked against the Jews, but the Germans were stirred up by Hitler to such an extent that they began to also threaten the Gentiles, especially the Catholics because Hitler believed that Catholicism was a part of Judaism. The Germans tried to cause a wide rift between Christians and their Jewish friends.

For a while, all regulations regarding Jews appeared in the newspapers. Later, after they found out where Jewish people lived, the Nazis issued all orders in writing, delivered to the homes of Jews.

One of the first orders to appear in the newspaper read as follows:

ALL JEWS LIVING ON THE COAST SINCE 1936 MUST LEAVE THEIR RESIDENCES IMMEDIATELY.

This included Felix's mother, his sister Nellie, and all refugees from Germany, Poland, and Austria who came to Holland after 1936. But where would they go? Felix's mother had just begun to settle in, and now we had to tell her that she must move again. It was heartbreaking to watch her cry bitterly when we told her; she just couldn't comprehend why.

During the time we learned that Felix's family would have to move, I suddenly got an idea and optimistically blurted out, "Let's take them to Amersfoort!"

At this, Felix's mother began to cry. In between her sobs she asked, "Where is Amersfoort? Where can we go? We don't know anyone in Amersfoort."

We patiently told her of my family in Amersfoort—my beloved Aunt Flora, after whom I was named, and my uncle, Jules Frank, in addition to my brother Ies and his wife. My aunt and uncle had lived there ever since they had married. My Aunt Flora was a warm and compassionate woman, filled with love for others and always eager to help. Uncle Jules was a dignified man, dedicated to the tenets of the Jewish religion and a prominent figure on the board of the local synagogue.

Felix's mother and sister reluctantly packed some suitcases, and later that week we hired a taxi. My mother and I accompanied them to Amersfoort, where my family warmly welcomed them.

Though it was nice to be together with my family again and to see my brother and sister-in-law, it was difficult to fake a festive mood. My aunt and uncle lived in a small but lovely home surrounded by canals and other natural beauty, and usually whenever we came to their home a sense of peace and warmth came over us. They lived harmoniously for many years at this house, Joannes van Dieststraat No. 13. Their pet chicken named Jamsje had the run of the house and often dominated the family.

But of course this trip to their home did not produce the same sense of peacefulness because now we saw things with different eyes. I felt that Felix's mother was not comprehending everything, and in a sense I thought that was good. After all, Holland, for her, was still a strange country, and the language was difficult to understand. We tried to keep her from listening to the radio, on which all day long Germans boasted of their victories or berated the Jews, whom they said would soon be eradicated. The two brothers, Theo and Felix, set out to find a place for Nellie and their mother. Within a few days they had located a furnished home on a nice street in Amersfoort, called the Rubensstraat.

After everyone was settled, Theo, Felix, my mother, and I went back to Rotterdam. Theo and Felix resumed their positions in the offices of their grain business. For a while life seemed to have calmed down, but we still held onto our disgust and fear of the Germans, who were taking possession of our country. During this time, the SS and the Gestapo rooted themselves in Holland. The stolid expressions on their faces and the power they wielded predicted what the future would hold for the Jews.

For some reason I began to cut out and save newspaper articles concerning Jews. I hid these clippings deep in my closet where my mother would not find them.

All of us lived in fear and panic. We tried frantically to obtain visas for other countries, which was just about unthinkable because of what Hitler's blitzkrieg had already done in Europe.

The real terror began in September 1940, followed by almost five years of unspeakable atrocities and crimes of torment for the Jewish population. Now we truly began to live in the Valley of Death.

CHAPTER 5

The Persecution Begins

Photo taken just before Felix and I leave Holland

The month of September 1940 began with a series of unending ordinances directed at the Jews. They were called, in Dutch, "Bekendmaking Voor Joden" (loosely translated, Summons for Jews). They always ended with the following:

ALL JEWS WHO DO NOT ADHERE TO THESE SUMMONS WILL BE ARRESTED AND SENT TO THE CONCENTRATION CAMP IN MAUTHAUSEN.

I remember the first order, or summons, was that every Jew had to report to the local district locale to sign important papers to indicate whether they were fully Jewish, half Jewish, or one-quarter Jewish; how far back their Jewish ancestry could be traced; how many grandparents from either side of the family were Jewish; and so on. We were even asked about the ethnicity of our great-grand-parents. If a Christian man was married to a Jewish woman, or vice versa, there was talk of sterilization.

The Nazis were insanely preoccupied with these kinds of matters because they were obsessed with keeping the Aryan race free of any Jewish blood. And like frightened sheep, we all followed each other to obey these bizarre ordinances.

Shortly after this particular summons, another one appeared in the papers. It ordered all Jews to appear at a certain place to have their photograph taken. The instructions read: "The left ear has to be exposed; women, no earrings, hair combed back." With much sadness in our hearts, we obeyed the ordinance. A German took our photograph, then attached it to a booklet stamped with a J for Jew (*Jood* in Dutch). The Germans thought that the names "Sara" and "Israel" were uniquely Jewish, so in each booklet the name Sara was printed before each woman's first name and Israel before each man's first name. This document was called, in Dutch, *Persoonsbewijs*, meaning "identification certificate." We had to carry this with us at all times.

There was an area in Amsterdam called the Jordaan, where many working-class Jews lived harmoniously with non-Jewish working-class people. The Nazis did not like the close relationships between Jews and Gentiles in the Jordaan, so they often instigated riots by heckling the Jewish people. This heckling led to a terrible revolt by the Gentiles against the Nazis. The Christian population went on strike in Amsterdam and surrounding areas. People stopped going to work in factories, retail stores, and other places of business. The Germans needed these people to support their war machine, and now everything stood still. The strike took place around February 25, 1941; as we understood it, this was the first protest against one of the most powerful enemy occupations in history.

The Dutch did not give up easily, but they were powerless against the Germans. When the Germans began capturing and killing Jews, the non-Jewish strikers screamed, "We want our Jews; leave our Jews alone!" Hundreds of Christian protesters were killed during this strike, which lasted several days. This event of the Nazi occupation in Holland is written in blood. We must forever remember the moral courage of the non-Jewish people in Holland.

Meanwhile, the English began to attack the Germans, and so we had English and German fighter planes waging a war over our heads. There were continuous air raids. During this time the Germans initiated a crafty plan. They appointed a body of prominent Jewish people in Amsterdam, which they called De Joodse Raad, meaning "the Jewish Council." It was headed by the industrialist Mr. A. Asscher and by Professor Dr. D. Cohen. The Germans promised these members of the Jewish Council that they would be in charge of all Dutch Jewish affairs in Holland in connection with Nazi ordinances. At least that's what they were told—and it is what they naively believed. Now, heinous actions by the occupying forces quickly followed one after the other. The Jewish Council had the dubious task of urging all Jewish people to register with them in Amsterdam, thinking that they could trust the Germans if they cooperated with them.

One day at the beginning of 1941 my mother said to me, "Why don't you go to the zoo to get your mind off things." We had been members of the Rotterdam Zoo for as long as we had lived there, and it was not far from our home. I was always exceptionally fond of animals, so I was elated to learn that the zoo had been restored and reopened after the invasion. I got on my bike and rode to the Rotterdam Zoo. When I arrived I parked my bike in the bike rack and walked over to the entrance.

To my great disgust, I came upon a large sign with bold lettering that stated, Voor Joden Verboden. This means "forbidden for Jews." I must have stood there for a long, long time reading and rereading the sign. I was horrified; it was like a knife through my heart. For a moment I thought, "I will go in anyway; what do those animals know?" But I remembered the dreaded document stamped with the letter J deep in my pocket. I dared not go in.

After this demeaning experience I rode my bike to my aunt and uncle's home to see how they were doing. My aunt was still under medical care, and she looked miserable. But at least she was home and could move around a bit. My favorite cousin, Jacob, and my uncle were also home. My uncle had never been a big talker, but after I had told him what had happened at the zoo, he said, "Prepare yourself; this is just the beginning. No good can be expected."

After my visit I rode home. I kept myself occupied with cutting out all of the ordinances that appeared in the newspapers. I hid them in my closet and cried. My mother asked me, "Whatever are you always cutting out?" Because I did not want to upset her, I ignored her question and changed the subject.

Signs reading Forbidden for Jews began to appear all over. Jews were no longer allowed in parks, theaters, or schools. In front of

the home where the famous painter Rembrandt van Rijn had lived
in Amsterdam was a sign that read, Jews Are Forbidden Here! Jews
were not even allowed in the center of Amsterdam. In addition,
the Germans mandated a separation between Jews and non-Jews:
it was absolutely forbidden for the Jewish population to mingle
with Christians.

In this year, 1941, many Jewish couples began to leave their
babies on the doorsteps of Christian homes, churches, and con-
vents. But the Germans immediately stopped this by putting bold
ordinances in the newspapers, stating the following:

**ALL CHILDREN AND BABIES LEFT OR FOUND
AT DOORSTEPS OF NON-JEWISH HOMES
AND CHURCHES ARE DECLARED JEWISH AND
WILL BE SENT TO MAUTHAUSEN.**

In our Dutch way of thinking, it was unbelievable that we
were to be put in concentration camps. Many families preferred
death over living with this prospect.

There was a Jewish weekly newspaper in Holland called *Het
Nieuw Israelitiesch Weekblad*. In 1941 this newspaper was banned
by the Germans and replaced by another, called the *Jewish Weekly*,
which was nothing more than a vehicle in which the Germans printed
their regulations and ordinances. Soon Jews had to turn in their radios and bicycles, and they were not allowed to have telephones in
their homes. They were absolutely forbidden to enter the homes of
non-Jewish people.

At that time I had not heard of Mauthausen. I looked it up in
my atlas and found that it was located somewhere in Austria. At

first—as I understood it—it served as a concentration camp for anti-Nazis; later it was the camp most dreaded by the Dutch Jewish people. Mauthausen was reputed to be a labor camp run under the most atrocious conditions. People who had the unfortunate fate to end up there never came back, whether they were Jews or non-Jews. It is said that the commander of this camp, Franz Ziereis, gave his son for his birthday fifty Jews for target shooting practice.

We still lived in our flat in Rotterdam, though we could not communicate with the family. There was danger everywhere. One day my Uncle Saam came to our home unexpectedly. He had aged drastically. Instead of the tall, handsome, impressive man that I remembered, I saw a shrunken old gentleman with a face full of sorrow. He said, "I want to know, first of all, how you both are doing, and then I have to tell you something important."

We talked a bit, and of course the conversation focused on what was happening to the Jewish population. Although my father's side of the family had not been very religious, they all knew they were Jewish. My uncle said, looking at no one in particular, "You see, things are getting worse and worse for the Jews; don't you see we have reached the point of no return? I discussed the whole situation with Aunt Sophie and the girls, and we have decided to convert to Christianity, you see. If we become Christians, you see, we might not fall prey to the Germans." My mother and I could not believe what we were hearing. He continued, "We have dear friends in the Christian community, you see, and we are going to convert to Catholicism."

My mother, moderate as she always was, said nothing. But I said, "But, Uncle, what about your name, Cohen? It sounds pretty Jewish."

I could see that he had anticipated our reaction, but he said, "I feel it is my duty to do everything possible to save our lives." There was silence for a long time, and I expected him to advise us to do the same thing. But that did not happen.

Finally my mother broke the silence and said, "Well, I really wish and hope that it is for your good."

In my ignorance I said, "How does that work? Do you now have to wear a cross?"

But my uncle did not go into details. He said to us, "Sophie and the girls wish you good luck; you see, maybe the war will be over soon." In my youthful imagination I pictured my aunt and uncle kneeling in a church and making the sign of the cross; I figured that they had to do something about the last name of Cohen.

My mother said, "We are living in such a bizarre time, nothing surprises me anymore. Let's wish them good luck and forget about it."

That night in bed I kept thinking about our lives and especially how my uncle's decision would work out. I had been very close with my cousin Lenie, my aunt and uncle's youngest daughter, and wondered what her fate would be with her new religion. After the war I learned that my aunt and uncle, their oldest daughter, and her husband all perished at the hands of the Nazis. Their two grandchildren survived. My cousin Lenie survived in a convent. She remained a Catholic.

<hr />

The High Holy Days in the fall of 1940 came and went without, of course, the usual feeling of solemnity. My mother bravely walked to the local synagogue on the day of Rosh Hashanah, but I preferred to stay home. I only accompanied my mother on the Day of Atonement, the Yom Kippur Holy Day. It was a long distance to walk from our home to the synagogue, inevitably encountering German soldiers, who were up to no good. I thought it ludicrous to go to the temple, but I went for the sake of my mother.

The festivals following the High Holy Days—Sukkot, Simchat Torah, and Hanukkah—normally such happy days, were spent at home. I kept thinking with nostalgia about the festival of Sukkot, so called to remind us of the Jews' exodus out of Egypt. This year the holidays were filled with anxiety and fear. My mother tried to retain some semblance of the way we had celebrated Friday night Shabbat in the past. She would place a white tablecloth on our table, prepare some special dishes, and try to put on a happy face, saying to me, "Let's say a prayer." The ritual always ended with Kaddish.

Often, looking at the three suitcases we had packed "in case of," I said to my mother, "I wonder if the prayers will do any good."

My mother would reply, "The war will be over soon."

Alone in bed at night, I would hold a monologue with God, who now, in my mind, had become a stranger, someone who did not care any longer, someone who had abandoned us. It was very confusing for me.

One day in the spring of 1941, an ordinance appeared in the newspaper stating that all Jews still living on the shoreline had to leave their homes immediately. We were to leave our pets behind. We were to pick up maps to see which cities were affected by this ordinance. Rotterdam, of course, was affected; it was the largest and most important harbor in Europe, if not the world.

But where to? Amersfoort, of course, the most significant town in our lives. We immediately got in touch with my aunt, uncle, and cousins in Rotterdam, who also were at their wits' end. They told us that friends had offered them a place to stay for the time being. Some friends within Felix's circle of acquaintances had suggested that we go into hiding. But how could we go into hiding in Holland, a small country, as flat as a pancake?

The Jewish people in Holland were further ordered by the German authorities to leave everything behind and turn in house keys to a particular German office. Pets would be destroyed. If these orders were not followed by a certain date, transgressors would be arrested and sent to Mauthausen. And so our three "in case of" suitcases became useful, after all.

Jewish people had to turn in their radios in April of 1941. In one respect, we were glad that we no longer had to listen to the blarings of Seyss-Inquart, Rauter, and Aus der Funten, who assured the Dutch population in their speeches that they would soon get rid of the Jews.

The Germans had already begun to confiscate all Jewish businesses and corporations. They simply sent out letters notifying the owners and presidents of these companies that their businesses were now in the hands of a German *Verwalter*, meaning "manager" or "administrator." The German administrator would arrive; seize all books, papers, bank deposits, and other important information; then promptly fire all Dutch employees. Among the hundreds of newspaper clippings and documents that I hid during those years was the following letter of dismissal sent to Felix by the German *Verwalter*:

REGISTERED LETTER

In regards to ordinance #198 by the High Commissioner of
the occupied Dutch territories, I have been ordered to inform
you that you have been dismissed from your position with the
N.V. Nidera Handelscompagnie, Rotterdam, as of immediately. Please acknowledge receipt of this letter. On behalf of
the High Commissioner of the occupied Dutch territory, Dr.
Arthur Seyss-Inquart.

Felix and his brother Theo had to stay in Rotterdam for a while
because they were required to "assist" in liquidating the company
and showing the German administrator the ropes.

My mother and I packed a few more items, and I made sure
that I took all of my newspaper clippings with me to Amersfoort.
We had a cat named Mimi, which we gave to our neighbors, who
assured us that they would take good care of her. Valuable items
such as paintings, silver, flatware, china, and anything that was too
heavy to carry had to be left behind. The Germans would then have
access to our precious belongings.

Of course, we were welcomed with open arms by my brother
Ies and his wife as well as our other family members. But all of us
felt aimless and hopeless because we were now venturing through
a labyrinth of hell that we could not understand. We had lost contact with our family in Rotterdam; everyone was going in different
directions, not knowing what to do. We all knew that a disaster
would follow, an unknown but terrible fate, an Armageddon.

It so happened that my brother Ies had Christian friends who
owned a bookstore. The owner was ill; his wife was also ailing. Upon
hearing of our fate, this couple immediately offered my mother and

me the entire second floor of their property, fully furnished, free of rent, in exchange for help in their bookstore.

The arrangement worked out well, but we felt guilty living there because we were not supposed to mingle with non-Jewish people. We also noticed that these good people were not aware of—or perhaps did not pay attention to—the endless ordinances and regulations that appeared in the newspapers.

One day a German officer came into the bookstore and looked around. He then turned to me and said that we had to make sure that no books by Jewish authors were carried in the store any longer. He never asked me to produce my papers. Inwardly, I was shaken terribly. He left, clicking his heels. It was such an awful experience for me that I had to discuss this situation with the owner, telling him that I could no longer work in his bookstore. He and his wife felt very sorry about this because the arrangement had been working out so well for all of us. Consequently, my mother and I had to look for another place to live.

We were able to find a small but neatly furnished place on the same street where Nellie, Felix's sister, and her mother lived in the Rubensstraat. After Felix and Theo "assisted" the German administrator in liquidating the family business, they too moved in with their mother and sister. And so for the time being our families found some consolation in each other's company.

Every regulation from the Germans was, of course, a threat and was intended to produce a vicious cycle of problems for the Jewish people. We could not live a normal life. For example, after taking away businesses from Jews, the Germans issued a new ordinance stating that Jews who were unemployed would be sent to camps to work for the Germans.

One evening my brother Ies and I attended a concert in the music hall in Amersfoort when suddenly, upon orders of the local German commandant, we heard a voice over the loudspeaker ordering all Jews in attendance to leave immediately. Every person in the concert hall that evening left in solidarity with their Jewish compatriots.

Jewish professionals such as attorneys, doctors, pharmacists, notaries, midwives, and a host of other highly trained professionals were no longer allowed to work. Jewish people were no longer allowed to go to public places such as parks, hotels, restaurants, swimming pools, concert halls, libraries, and museums. No Jew could continue to be a member of a tennis club, football team, bridge team, or even a group of fishing buddies. We could not even enter beauty parlors or barber shops any longer.

The Jewish community in Amersfoort had always been close with the non-Jewish community. But now, with one ordinance, this was all over.

+≻═══≺+

The non-Jewish population was, of course, also suffering at the hands of the Nazis. They too had to follow all kinds of absurd regulations, which were always accompanied by threats. For example, schools were no longer allowed to teach students about world history, particularly World War I, which the Germans had lost. In addition, anything pertaining to the royal family was strictly forbidden to appear in textbooks. Photographs of Queen Wilhelmina, her daughter, Princess Juliana, Juliana's husband, Prince Bernhard, or their children were not allowed to be seen anywhere—all pictures were to be destroyed. Indications that there ever was a royal family in Holland were forbidden.

One would have thought that the Germans had plenty of other things to contend with. But I do believe that their power was laced with sadistic tendencies, and they took great pleasure in evil acts against citizens. Teachers were ordered, with many threats, to carry out these ordinances. Ironically, these orders produced just the opposite: by drawing attention to these changes, the history of Holland and information about the Royal House of Nassau was reinforced. We knew anyway that Queen Wilhelmina was in England and that the princess and her children were in Canada.

Even streets that had been named after the Royal House had to be changed, and streets named after Jewish painters, writers, scientists, and other prominent people were eliminated altogether. Holland was robbed of honoring those who had contributed much to its culture and history.

Food also became scarce because the Germans took away anything they could get their hands on, "upon orders of the Führer." They stole works of art, clothing, shoes, and other goods and sent everything to their *Heimat*, their homes in Germany. They looted constantly. If the Germans did not want the Dutch to see what they were doing, they simply placed signs up that read

PEOPLE WILL BE SHOT HERE WITHOUT WARNING.

The floor that we occupied on the Rubensstraat was owned by a young couple, Jan and Eefje Kolkman, who had two small children.

They were very nice, patriotic people and allowed us to use their telephone and other facilities. Jan was involved with one of the resistance movements that had sprung up shortly after the German invasion. He had a crystal radio on which he could listen to the BBC, the *Voice of the Free World*. At night we would come together and learn what really went on. Queen Wilhelmina, now in exile in England, spoke often on this radio program and sent encouraging words of hope to her former subjects in Holland to remain steadfast (Je Maintiendrai).

The citizens who joined these resistance movements were people of great courage. They were not afraid to take risks for their own lives or for the lives of their families. We learned during the course of the war that great numbers of patriots had been killed by the Nazis. At that time we were not familiar with the operations of the resistance movements, but Jan told us all they had accomplished. Thanks to the bravery of people in the resistance, bridges, railroads, and other important transportation and communications that were of value to the German war machine were destroyed or made unusable for the Germans.

During the time we lived with the young couple, we learned of events that would never be written about in the Nazi-controlled newspapers. Jan brought us newspapers printed by the resistance movements in which their articles urged the Jewish people not to obey orders from the Germans. It was also strange to read in these resistance papers that we should ignore orders from the Jewish Council, who continued to urge the Jewish population to come and register their addresses.

Of course, the vast majority of Jewish people believed in and followed orders from the Jewish Council because they were convinced that the council knew what was best for us. Felix, however, believed that the council advisers were ignorant men and that the organization was laced with stupidity and blind to the true purposes of the Nazis, into whose hands the Jewish Council played. It turned out later that Felix was right. For example, there was a well-known bank in Amsterdam called Lippmann-Rosenthal, originally owned by German Jews. The bank had been taken over by the Nazis; however, the name of the bank was kept the same to fool the Jewish people into thinking that it was still run by Jewish business people.

One day the following ordinance appeared in the newspapers:

ALL ITEMS OF GOLD, SUCH AS GOLD COINS, JEWELRY, OR ANY OTHER ARTICLES OF GOLD OR ANTIQUES, MUST BE TURNED IN BY JEWS TO THE LIPPMANN-ROSENTHAL BANK IN AMSTERDAM.

The ordinance stated a deadline for turning in these items as well as the address of the bank. Felix's brother Theo, who was gullible, immediately went to Amsterdam and turned in all of his gold coins and other valuables. Felix and I, of course, had nothing to turn in, since all that we had owned was now at the bottom of the North Sea.

By now the Germans had the addresses of a great many Jewish people, which they had gotten from the Jewish Council. Orders from the Nazis now came directly to our homes via registered mail, and the Nazis saw to it that these ordinances arrived on the evenings or days of the Shabbat as well as other Jewish Holy Days, especially during Passover, because they knew we would be at home. Felix visited us every night after dark. He frequently said, "I will never register in Amsterdam. Never! Never!"

One evening our neighbor and landlord, Jan, came rushing to our room. It was June 22, 1941. He said in an excited voice, his face flushed from exertion, "Guess what ... good news ... I heard on the crystal ... can you believe it? Germany attacked Russia!" He continued with a wide grin on his face, "Boy, oh, boy, that will be the end of the master race!"

We became swept up in Jan's enthusiasm. Our excitement continued as Felix entered the room. Felix too was excited, but he remained more objective than the rest of us. Jan continued, "This is the beginning of the end for the Germans; you better believe it. Nobody has ever conquered Russia. I don't know whether we will survive, but I can guarantee you here and now that the Germans will lose the war." And so the conversation went on and on that night; there was a flicker of hope for all of us.

Jan's wife Eefje had also come upstairs during our animated conversation, and together we celebrated the inevitable downfall—we hoped and believed—of the German blitzkrieg and Hitler's master race. Felix, who was an expert in history, explained his view. He said, "We can't say anything for sure yet, until the winter comes. Then we will see a victory, but there will be many casualties, I'm afraid."

Suddenly the newspapers were forbidden to write anything regarding Russian literature, Russian works of art, or Russian culture. Now the Russians were the enemies of the Germans, whereas before they were partners in war.

And so we spent many evenings together, we three families, all of us hopeful. Jan told us about the resistance and how its members— on many occasions—were successful in fooling the Germans. In the beginning of the resistance movements, their members had little experience in this type of war situation and many mistakes were made. Unfortunately, great numbers of these patriotic people were caught and killed.

The following is the text of an article that appeared in one of the underground newspapers that Jan had given us. The newspaper was called *De Waarheid,* meaning "The Truth."

> We find ourselves in the greatest and most heinous population destruction which the world has ever seen. There is no comparison with anything else than that which the Nazi tyranny has brought upon us. We do not want fascism in the Netherlands, no anti-Semitism, no oppression, no German poison. We abhor racial hatred. CITIZENS: PROTEST.

Our fear for Jan was continuous. He told us so many secrets, such as the way the resistance movements made false food coupons, how they circulated all the underground newspapers, and how they knew how to set up secret connections with people in London. We emphasized to Jan and his wife Eefje to be careful, but they were young and enthusiastic for their cause and therefore saw no danger.

One day I said to my mother, "I am going to the post office to mail a letter."

That special, worried look came over my mother's face as she asked me, "What letter, and to whom are you sending it?"

I answered, "Well, you know, to the Schepenstraat. I want to find out where Aunt Sien and the family are."

Against my mother's protest I left the house. When I arrived at the post office, I did not see many people other than a German soldier standing near the entrance. I needed a stamp, so I went to the service window and asked the clerk for one. The clerk looked me over and said, "You have to first fill out a form." I looked quite puzzled, and a feeling of claustrophobia came over me. The clerk continued, "Are there any pictures in the letter, and did you write it in German?" He took the letter in his hands and, looking me over again, said, "The letter has to be open, and you cannot have any crossword puzzles or chess problems or music in it." He then handed the letter back to me.

I backed up a bit and started to tear up the letter. I was about to run away when he motioned me to come to another window. Somehow I had a feeling that he was a good, patriotic citizen and that he wanted to tell me something important. He said, "Don't you know all about the new rules coming out?" His voice was almost a whisper. "The Germans want to know everything, the names and addresses of the senders, what you are writing about. You are not allowed to put the letters in the mailbox anymore. You have to show your papers." He went on and on in his low voice.

By that time the German soldier had obviously become suspicious. He walked toward us, but I could see that he did not understand our language. I could see that he was not too bright either. The clerk ended our conversation with, "You better go home fast."

I ran out of the post office with the torn-up pieces of the letter in my coat pocket. Luckily I reached my home safely. I realized then that I had only narrowly escaped. There were many, many more narrow escapes to come.

+=====+

My sister, Elisabeth, had become a companion to a family with whom she lived in Amersfoort. Elisabeth was extremely nervous as a result of all the horrible things that were going on. Each time that we saw her she said, "If we die, we will see each other in the hereafter." Her mind had been filled with these thoughts since the time of the invasion when the Germans rang our doorbell for utensils.

In the meantime, Felix's sister, Nellie, had met a young man who also was a refugee from Germany. He and his mother, who was sickly, lived not far from us for Amersfoort, at that time, was still a small town. I divided my time as best I could among all my family and friends.

All of us felt dazed and bewildered; everything we did seemed aimless. Whenever we got together we talked about our lovely country, Holland, and how it had become a theater of hell. We knew that we could not expect anything good in the future with the Germans in charge, especially when we read in the newspapers how they planned to eradicate the Jewish population.

A tiny flicker of hope came one day in the winter of 1941, when Felix received a letter from the German consul's office indicating that we could get our exit visas to immigrate to Cuba. Shortly after the invasion, Felix had gone to the German consulate to apply for us and several family members for exit visas. We were willing to go anywhere. For a year we had not heard a word from the consulate's office regarding our applications, but now this letter reached us from the German Immigration Department. At the time we truly believed that this was our opportunity to escape the Nazis.

The letter directed us to come to a special office in Amsterdam that was set up solely for Jewish people. The letter included a great number of instructions as to what to bring with us: passports, X-rays, family history, and a certain amount of money. Frantically, we gathered everything together for the appointed time. When all of this was done, Nellie, her boyfriend Kurt, Felix, and I set off by train to Amsterdam.

I had a terrible, sleepless night the night before we left, with nightmares and stomach upsets. Deep in my heart I felt that no good would come of this; once again, I had that feeling of impending doom. But outwardly I kept my calm.

When we arrived at the office in Amsterdam, we were ordered to stand on a yellow painted line. We were forbidden to speak. A lot of other Jewish people had also come to get a visa to exit Holland. The officials made us stand there on that yellow line for a long, long time. Upon seeing the swastikas and Nazi flags, we almost wanted to turn back. When our turn finally came, I looked at the German official sitting behind the window. Never in my life had I seen such hatred in anyone's eyes.

After questioning us extensively, the official handed us a document stating that Cuba had confirmed an entry visa for us. We had to pay a sum of money for which we received a confirmation. Finally, the four of us left Amsterdam with our documents in hand. They had kept our passports, informing us that they would be mailed to us after Berlin had confirmed our arrangements.

When we arrived home and analyzed the situation, we came to the conclusion that it would have been better had we not gone to Amsterdam at all. As it turned out, we never received our passports in the mail, nor did we hear from Cuba. The Germans had simply gotten richer from all the money they had collected from the Jewish people.

We discussed our experiences with the family and with the Kolkmans, our neighbors downstairs. Jan remarked, "How could you have gone? You know that you cannot trust the Germans. All they want is your money."

There was not much information broadcast on the crystal radio about the fate of our Jewish brothers and sisters in other countries occupied by the Germans. We could only guess their future by what we were experiencing in Holland. So far, the news from the "free world" did not include any news about the treatment of the Jews.

All we heard on the Nazi-controlled radio was continuous boasting by the Germans of their victories, speeches by Seyss-Inquart that soon the war would be over and that Hitler would accomplish a total victory with the annihilation of all Jews. But we also heard on Jan's crystal radio that at some date in 1941, the British had destroyed the large German battleship, the *Bismarck*. The Dutch press was not allowed to say much about it in the newspapers, so information was limited to only a few lines.

I often visited my aunt and uncle, Isse and Serien van Zuiden. It always gave me a lift to be with them in their elegant shop. Their living quarters were upstairs over their boutique, which was quite customary in Holland during those times. Their shop was not too far from where I lived, and I walked there and spent days helping them out, sorting through merchandise, and returning dresses to the racks.

One day a heartbreaking tragedy took place. We discovered a huge swastika at the entrance to the store. My uncle, in his innocence, said, "We have to clean it up immediately." I went to get a broom from the back of the closet, and then we diligently began to try to remove it. Suddenly, an SS official stormed in from nowhere, shouting in German to both my uncle and me; then he attacked my uncle with a heavy object. My aunt and I began to scream, but we were powerless to help. Several of Hitler's SS army men dragged my uncle away, and we learned he was taken to the concentration camp in Amersfoort.

The rabbi of the Jewish community and many of our friends tried desperately to get my uncle back home. After six weeks in the concentration camp he did come home, a broken man with many serious head wounds. My aunt and family tried to nurse my uncle back to some physical recovery. But a short time later the Nazis came to take him back to the camp, where they immediately beat him to death.

This heinous incident had a devastating effect not only on my relatives, and especially my aunt, but also on the entire Jewish community in Amersfoort. The boutique was closed; it never opened again.

When we talked to Felix and his family the night after my uncle was killed, Felix said, "The enormity of the tragedies that the Germans will bring upon us is not fully understood by the Dutch. The Jewish Council still thinks it is doing us a favor by accommodating and cooperating with the Germans. All of us are doomed if we don't get out of here. I will fight to the last minute."

My uncle was fifty-six years old when he died. I grieved for him; I grieved for humanity. I grieved for our future. I realized that with the Germans in my country, everything we had known—culture, refinement, civility—was gone.

CHAPTER 6

The Deportations

Felix's mother

The pogroms and deportations began. Our world as we knew it was gone. Ghettos were created by the Nazis, first in the big cities. Entire areas were fenced in and staked out with large signs, printed with big letters that read, JEWISH AREA ONLY. Jewish people were not allowed to leave their homes between 6:00 p.m. and 6:00 a.m. We were required to put signs on our homes that read, Jewish Locale.

My mother and I should not have been residing in a non-Jewish home. This provoked the utmost fear within us. But the Kolkmans were not afraid of the Germans and in typical Dutch fashion told us, "Don't pay attention to the *Rot-Moffen*," which means, "those crazy Germans."

Although we had been aware of the systematic eradication of the Jewish population in Germany, I felt that the evil forces of the German occupation were not completely understood by us innocent, and somewhat gullible, Dutch Jews. We still underestimated the evil of the Nazis. Soon, however, we realized what the Germans were capable of. They began to pick up people right from the streets of the cities; then they tortured and killed them. It seemed their actions depended upon their moods, and they did not have to account for their evil crimes to anyone. Until the deportations began, the suicides among the Jewish people grew to epidemic proportions.

On December 7, 1941, Jan ran up the stairs to our place, his eyes almost bulging from their sockets. His face was flushed with excitement as he said, "I just heard on my crystal that the Japanese bombed Pearl Harbor. It is a terrible disaster for the Americans. I am sure that America will now get into the war."

We spent the entire evening talking about the bombing of Pearl Harbor and guessing what might happen next. The following morning we learned that the United States had declared war on Japan, after which Germany declared war on the United States. The Germans and the Japanese had now become partners in evil. Again, we became swept up in Jan's enthusiasm. We were certain that the Germans would lose the war. But when? And would it be too late for the Jewish people?

The Germans became much bolder and no longer committed their crimes in secret. Right after the United States became embroiled in the war, Seyss-Inquart gave an abominably long speech directed at America and, once again, Jews. His speech appeared

on the front pages of all of the newspapers. He claimed that the
United States would "spend milliards and milliards," which translated means "billions and billions of dollars," but would lose the war
anyway. He went so far as to accuse the Jews of causing the tragedy
at Pearl Harbor and claimed that Jews ruined patriotism throughout the world. Seyss-Inquart assured his listeners that Germany would
destroy American ships. He ended his speech with "Germany will win
for the entire world."

I am not sure of the exact origin of the word *razzia*, but it carried a meaning of doom. It meant "roundup" or a "raid on suspects."
It certainly meant death for us. Between the hours of curfew, the
razzias began. The Germans would enter certain areas where Jews
resided, herd them up, throw them into trucks, and deport them to
Westerbork, the dreaded processing camp in the north of Holland.
It made no difference to the Germans if the Jews were old or sick.
If the elderly were bedridden, the Nazis used water hoses to make
them get out of bed or dogs who were trained to viciously bite
people. Then the Nazis dragged these critically ill and injured
people into the trucks.

The homes of these Jews were then sealed, and the Germans had
the freedom to steal whatever they fancied. There was a foreman of
the SS in Holland by the name of J. H. Feldmeyer. It was widely
known that after rounding up Jewish people and deporting them, he
helped himself to valuable items in their homes: art, antiques, jewelry, and even furniture, which he shipped off to Germany.

Many protest letters by Catholic clergy were addressed to Seyss-
Inquart, to Rauter, and to other high officials in the German occu-

pation. As a result of these protests, hundreds of Catholics were deported to Germany to "work for the war machine." Most of them never returned. Non-Jews were strictly prohibited from entering Jewish areas, which were partitioned by barbed wire.

In the meantime, everyone in Holland suffered from continuous air raids. Allied planes sometimes hit civilian areas, and innocent people were killed. Jan told us how, on many occasions, the resistance movements came to the aid of the British pilots whose planes had been shot down. The underground movements became more and more experienced in eluding the Nazis. They were not afraid to act quickly in dangerous situations.

Felix still had cousins living in the outskirts of Rotterdam with whom his brother Theo had contact. The husband had been the head of the grain company where Felix and Theo had been employed. In December of 1941 we learned from Theo that it might be possible for his cousins—and also for Theo—to escape Holland through Switzerland. This possibility did not seem a reality at first. One did not know what to think or what the next minute would bring. But as luck—or perhaps fate—would have it, Theo and the family made it over the Dutch border early in 1942. Felix's mother prayed day and night, not knowing how to cope with the emptiness that Theo's departure had left behind.

The cousins had lived for years in a stately home, which was elegantly furnished. The home featured a collection of some of the most breathtaking paintings and art objects. Felix had told me, before his brother and this family had escaped, that he would try to save the contents of the house. I paid little attention to this;

I was very distraught over the disappearance of several Jewish people I had known well who had been taken during the night by the Nazis, never to be seen or heard from again.

But when Theo and his cousins fled Holland, Felix arranged for the owner of a moving company in Amersfoort, a patriotic person, to help him load many of the valuables from the home into the truck. This was a daring venture and placed Felix in great risk. If someone had noticed him, or betrayed him, it would have been the end of his life. But Felix and his friend succeeded in loading the truck with as much as they could and transporting it to Amersfoort in good condition. The valuables were hidden in a secret place in the owner's home in Amersfoort. And, of course, we were overjoyed that Felix was safe.

When I told my mother what Felix had done, she turned white. "I'm glad that you didn't tell me," she said. "But what we should do now is pack some suitcases again with all the photographs and our belongings." Her face was forlorn. "I will ask the Kolkmans if we could leave everything here," she continued, "in case something should happen to us and we have to go." Her words, "in case we have to go," haunted me. I heard no hope in her voice, only surrender.

+⊱⋅⊰+

The deportations continued, and many of our family and friends disappeared. The ultimate degradation came in May 1942.

All Jewish people were ordered to wear the Star of David. We were ordered to appear in person at an office in Amersfoort to pick up and pay for the Stars of David, which were made of a dreadful yellow cloth. In the center of each star, in big, black letters, the word *Jew* was printed. Each Star of David came with instructions on how and where to put it on one's coat, dress, or suit so that it would be visible for anyone to see. Of course the instructions also came with the usual threats in the event that one did not adhere to the rules.

To protest this absurd situation, many Christian people also began to wear stars on their clothing. However, warnings immediately appeared in the newspapers informing the Christian population of the consequences that they would face should they continue to wear stars in protest. The Germans knew all too well how to instill fear in the hearts of people.

It seemed that the Germans felt it their right to detain anyone for any reason if he or she was wearing the Star of David. One never knew what would happen; so much depended on the temperament of the Nazi at the moment of detainment.

Following this latest order, my sister, Bep, came right away to the flat where we lived. She was terribly upset, and the anger in her eyes was like shooting fire. She blurted, "I will never wear that idiot star. Never! Never!" Looking at both my mother and me, my sister continued, "I am getting married to Abraham, and then we'll go into hiding. All of our Christian neighbors in the street are wearing the star just to pester those damned Germans." She continued with a flood of curses directed at the Germans.

My sister was very beautiful at the time. She had big blue eyes tinged with green, lovely golden brown hair, and peach skin, which most women from the northern countries were blessed with. She was a natural beauty. We had known for quite a while that she had become acquainted with a gentleman from the family where she had been staying. Mama and I had met him a number of times, and he struck us as a fine and intelligent man with a warm personality. He must have been at least twenty-five years older than she, and over the months that we knew him he had hinted several times to my mother that he would like to marry my sister.

My mother and I took in all of this; we were happy for my sister inasmuch as one could think of happiness at that time. My sister had never been a religious person. It had always been difficult to get her to go to synagogue, even under normal circumstances. But she said, "Abraham has contacted Mr. Van Dam; he will just marry us and then we will go into hiding."

We asked her, "Where will you go?"

She answered, "Oh, Abraham knows lots of farmers in Hoogland and Nijkerk. They will help us; I will leave it all up to Abraham."

Mr. Van Dam was our beloved rabbi. He functioned in Amersfoort as rabbi, cantor, Hebrew teacher, and besides all of this, inspector of ethnic foods to ensure that all were kosher, according to Jewish law.

As my sister continued her ranting, my mother interrupted her by saying, "You are an adult now, but remember, if you don't wear the star and they ask you for your papers, they will take you..."

My sister sneered, as if she was no longer afraid. She was probably strengthened by the prospect of getting married to someone who could make decisions for her. I kept my mouth shut during their conversation, but I was thinking, "With or without a star, the Nazis will do away with us in any case."

I got up from my chair and embraced my sister, wishing her well. My mother did the same. My sister then left with another stream of curses against the Germans.

We could not go to her wedding, which was just a quick formality; it was too dangerous for us to leave our house. I did not hear from my sister again until four years later, after the war. For my mother, it was the last time she embraced her daughter.

CHAPTER 7

The Hiding Years

*Although the photo is damaged, I treasure this picture
of Felix and me on our wedding day.*

It was now mid-June 1942. Early one morning Felix left for Amsterdam to try—in one last, frantic attempt—to get some papers from the Jewish Council for postponing deportation for ourselves and for both of our families. We had learned from the resistance movements, via the Kolkmans, that the offices of the Jewish Council were a madhouse. Jan told us that thousands of Jewish people stood in line for hours trying to register for extensions. The members of the council—honorable and deserving citizens, I am sure—were suddenly faced with totally unforeseen circumstances, having trusted the Germans on false promises that the council would be in charge of its own people. But now the council was at the mercy of monsters and beasts. There were rumors that by a certain date in the near future all Jews of Amersfoort would have to leave; Amersfoort was to become *Judenrein,* translated from the German, "cleansed of Jews."

Later that morning on the day that Felix left for Amsterdam, I received a dreadful announcement in the mail stating that I was required to report for work in Germany. The announcement listed the date and hour that I was to report to a train station in Hooghalen for a medical examination, which was to take place in the presence of the German police. I became almost hysterical.

The summons came from the Zentralstelle fur Judische Auswanderung, meaning, Central Office for Jewish Resettlement. The summons contained three pages. I was required to bring the following items with me:

- One suitcase
- One pair of boots
- One pair of stockings
- Two pieces of underwear
- One work outfit
- One sweater
- Two blankets
- Two sheets
- One plate, one drinking cup, one spoon
- One towel and some soap
- Enough food to last three days

I was also required to hand over food coupons at the station when I arrived.

Then came endless instructions on how to pack: a large suitcase was to be marked with my last name, first name, date of birth, and the word *Holland*. I was forbidden to take anything else from my home, and I was warned that pets were not allowed.

Then, with more threats came the following order: sickness was no excuse to ignore this ordinance. If a person was sick on the day of departure, then a German doctor would come for inspection along with the Gestapo. The summons continued with further orders: homes had to be locked up and keys put in one's travel bag. The summons had to be shown to the train personnel. The following items had to be packed in a separate bag:

- Bank accounts and bankbooks
- Savings accounts
- Stocks, bonds, and names of those who owed us money
- Life insurance, scholarship papers, and funeral funds with the location of the plots
- Credits from Holland or other countries
- Keys and numbers of safe deposit boxes
- Inheritances, interests from inheritances
- Rights of patents or real estate
- Art of any kind
- Collector's items
- Jewelry, diamonds, gold and/or silver objects, such as medals
- Any other valuables
- Gifts
- Transfers (promises for future gifts)
- Compensations from insurance companies
- A list of any debts
- Accurate descriptions of partnerships, with names, addresses, and telephone numbers of the partners
- Partnerships in land, real estate, and other business ventures
- Possessions or interests of any kind in provinces, cities, and/or any other country
- Mortgages
- Land registry numbers

At the bottom of page 3 of the summons, in large letters, it read:

**ON THE DAY OF YOUR DEPARTURE YOU WILL GET
A FREE TRAVEL PERMIT.**

**ANYONE NOT COMPLYING WITH THESE ORDERS
WILL BE HEAVILY PUNISHED.**

The summons was signed by SS Hauptsturmfuhrer Woerlein.

The shock I felt was indescribable. My mother and I clung together in desperation. Jan and Eefje came upstairs. They said to me,
"Don't go! We all know what this is all about. They cannot keep
track of everything and everyone."

I could not picture myself in a German camp working for the
German war efforts. I took the summons and put it in the bag with
my other papers, which I had carefully kept hidden. Somehow I
pretended, for my mother's sake, that I had never seen the summons, which was, of course, hiding my head like an ostrich. I did
not want my mother to know how deeply upset I was.

After the Kolkmans left I said to my mother, "There is hardly
anything to eat in the house. I have to go to the store and buy
some food."

My mother became alarmed and, embracing me, pleaded, "Please
don't go! With that star, they might pick you up." For a long while, we
remained in our mother-daughter embrace. In silence, our thoughts
were like windmills in a vicious storm.

+>——≺+

We did need something to eat, and I was adamant to get food.
Some stores were still open to Jewish people, but by orders from the

Germans, Jews could shop only on certain days of the week between the hours of three o'clock and five o'clock in the afternoon.

I waited until three o'clock; my heart was heavy with anxiety. The brilliant landscape of Holland, which I had so enjoyed in the past, with its cheerful homes, stately trees, picturesque bridges over elegant canals, and colorful flowers in full bloom, now looked terrifying to me. I saw everything with different eyes. Had it been nothing more than an optical illusion in the past? My heart was heavy, and fear was my constant companion during those years. Now I wondered if Felix would come back from Amsterdam and what would happen to his family.

I reached the store safely and bought what we needed. As I was leaving, that same strange and foreboding feeling overwhelmed me again. At first I hesitated, not leaving, but I had to go. I stood there for a while, thinking of the summons now hidden in my closet. I felt bewildered and forlorn.

Suddenly a tall man on his bicycle spotted me. He stopped, stepped off his bike, and approached me. He said, "What the hell are you doing here with that damned star on your blouse? Take that damned thing off and follow me." I had never seen this man before. He was very tall, a real sturdy Dutchman, fearless it seemed. For some reason I felt safe in his company; I instinctively knew I was in good hands.

I tore the star off my clothing and followed him. It was quite a long walk to his home. When we finally arrived, he motioned to me that I should go through the alley and wait for him while he parked his bike. After a few minutes he guided me through the backyard and into his home. He said, "I am Piet [pronounced Pete] Brandsen, and you are Jewish. Well, let's hear your story. What is your name? Where do you live?" As I began to talk, he interrupted and said, "Wait, let me call Dina." He removed the pipe he was smoking from his mouth and yelled, "Dina!"

Dina was his wife. I noticed immediately by the way she looked up at him that she adored him. She then looked at me and said hello. Piet said to Dina, "Get the girls here right away. I have an important matter to discuss." I heard Dina shout something out into the street, and shortly thereafter four girls came in. They all looked alike to me; all of them had white-blond hair and blue eyes.

Piet said to me, "These are our four girls. They are Beppie, who is five years old; Willie, who is seven; Henny, ten years old; and our oldest, Nel, who is twelve." In a very serious tone he commanded all of us: "Come upstairs, where we can talk. This is a serious matter." I could tell that all four children looked up to their father with deep respect. No matter that I had just met Piet. I knew right away that he was a man of few words. The tone of his voice and his entire demeanor were so effective that he had no need to repeat anything he said. We all went to one of the upstairs bedrooms.

He turned to his family and began. "Listen carefully. This is a Jewish girl, and we all know what will happen to the Jewish people with those damned Germans around." Upon hearing this, Dina made a sign of the cross, and so did the two older girls. Piet continued, "It is our duty to help. We must take her in and hide her." It sounded as simple as that! He then turned to me and said, "We want to hear your story. Tell us what is going on."

At first I was overwhelmed and speechless. Since there had not been much to eat lately, I became somewhat shaky and dizzy. My emotions, of course, contributed to my physical state. Piet pulled up some chairs. Dina and the four girls were sitting on the bed. And then I spoke freely. I told them that my mother and I lived with the Kolkman family in the Rubensstraat, that I had received the dreadful summons that morning, that I had a boyfriend who had gone to Amsterdam to try to get some extension papers. I explained that Felix and his family also lived in the Rubensstraat, that I did not know where my brother Ben or my sister were, or whether my oldest brother and his wife had gone into hiding. The words gushed out like a waterfall.

They all listened attentively. Piet smoked his pipe and appeared in deep thought. When I finished talking, he said, "I have heard of the Kolkmans; they are patriotic citizens." He then stood up and said, "I will take you home, but I will come back to your house tomorrow morning to speak with your mother and the other family." Turning to Dina and his daughters, in a stern voice he admonished them, "You are not to talk to anyone about this. If things leak out, all of us will be shot."

On our way home I told him about the shipwreck and how we had spent so many months in the hospital in England. He said to me, "You would have been smart to stay there."

When we were close to my home, I pointed out the house where Felix and his family lived. In a reassuring tone he said to me, "I will be there first thing in the morning. Bring everyone together, and we shall decide how to handle all of this." I thanked him profusely, and as we shook hands he said to me, "Someday we'll get rid of those damned *Rot-Moffen!*"

I rushed upstairs and noted with much gratitude in my heart that Felix had returned. He looked completely worn out. The people at the Jewish Council had been feverishly typing out requests and medical petitions for the sick and the old. Hundreds of people had stood in line for hours. Nurses from mental institutions had literally begged the Germans to allow ill patients, who could not work anyway, to stay in Holland.

The council staff had handed out blankets, warm coats, shoes, towels, bed linens, and other items for those who were destined for the camps. There were people who were old, young, and sick— in every physical condition. Felix met two young people who told him about their poor diabetic father whose leg had been amputated. During a razzia, the Nazis had dragged him out of bed and thrown him into a truck headed for one of the camps.

When the Germans had come, gathering people up with the clear intention of herding them off to concentration camps, Felix had fled. It had become too dangerous to stay any longer.

After Felix calmed down, I told him about my encounter with Piet Brandsen. After explaining everything, I told Felix that Piet would meet with all of us the next morning. Although we were in a deep state of despair and our moods were quite grave, for the moment we believed that not all was lost. Renewing our hopes, we looked forward to our meeting with Piet the next day.

+≻━≺+

Piet showed up the next morning, as promised. All of us met in Felix's home: Felix and his mother, Nellie and her boyfriend Kurt, and my mother and I were present. Piet radiated confidence, and I could tell that Felix and his family admired him. Our conversation focused on the German invaders, the eradication of the Jews wherever there was an occupation by Nazis, and our ideas on how long the war would last.

Piet told us that he was a contractor and involved in the resistance movement. He and his wife, both Catholics, believed it was their duty to help their fellow countrymen. He further explained that he had two rooms in the attic of his house; one was occupied by Dina's father, who was old and a bit senile. The other was available for us to hide in.

Then, after puffing on his pipe for a few long moments, he spoke to us in a very serious tone of voice. "I know that these are extraordinary times where quick action is required." Then, looking directly at Felix and me, he continued, "We are Catholics, and in our religion it is not right to have an unmarried couple in one room." There was silence for a few minutes. Then he said, "I would advise you to get married as soon as possible, and Dina and I will be happy to have you in our home. You don't have to worry about Dina's father. I will make up a story about who you are, in the event that the neighbors ask him."

Once again, I was faced with a spur-of-the-moment decision, just like the one I had made on the SS *Simon Bolivar*. Piet appeared quite calm even though this was a life-and-death matter. I knew that Felix loved me deeply. We had gone through so much together that it seemed the most natural thing in the world for us to get married before we went into hiding.

The first one to break the silence of the moment was Felix's mother, who was extremely Orthodox. She said in halting Dutch, "The rabbi, is he still here?" We looked at one another as she continued, "One has to be married by a rabbi in the synagogue."

Piet pointed out that this was not a time to think things over extensively or to make detailed plans. He said, "I know that Mr. Van Dam is the local Jewish spiritual leader. Let me find out what he can do, and I will come back later."

My mother was an easygoing person, and under these circumstances she understood that some religious customs had to be put aside. Felix's mother, however, attached much importance to the ways of her religion.

Piet left and promised to return soon. It seemed now that Felix and I were destined to be married. Felix, turning to his sister, Nellie, and her boyfriend, Kurt, said, "Perhaps Piet can help you also. If you have a chance to hide, don't let it slip away." But Kurt was hesitant; he still entertained illusions of escaping to Switzerland.

I suddenly began to feel very guilty. What about our mothers? Kurt also lived with his mother, who was sickly and a diabetic. Felix's mother began to cry. She said in German, "How can I stay behind alone?"

My mother said, "As long as I know that you and Felix are safe, I don't want you to worry about me." Our emotions were almost unbearable.

After a long two hours Piet returned. He regretfully reported that he had been unable to locate Mr. Van Dam. Before the invasion there had been four chief rabbis in Holland, one for each of four districts that consisted of certain provinces. Each rabbi—all of them learned scholars and renowned people—functioned as judge in religious matters or in special situations. In the district of Amersfoort, a certain Honorable Justus Tal, a well-known scholar, had been serving the Jewish communities for many years. His home was in Utrecht, a good-sized city located about twenty kilometers southwest of Amersfoort.

And so our conversation turned to Rabbi Tal. Piet stood up and said, "Listen, instead of spending valuable time trying to find out where Mr. Van Dam is, I will go and see if I can find Rabbi Tal, if he is still there. I will explain the situation to him. Give me the address of Rabbi Tal. I'll go to Utrecht and tell him what is going on."

When he was gone, our tension began to rise. Where would all of this lead to? What does one do in hiding? How long would we have to hide? What about our mothers, our families, our friends? Would we have enough food?

Early the next morning Piet returned. We all gathered again in Felix's home. There was Piet, pipe and all, our last-chance friend and hero. He told us that he had found Rabbi Tal at home—in his underwear. Rabbi Tal explained that the German "gentlemen" had robbed him of practically everything: his books, religious items, his robes, and his clothes. And Rabbi Tal still called the Nazis gentlemen!

The poor rabbi had listened carefully to Piet and then said, "By all means, the young couple must be saved." Understanding that there was not much time to waste and aware of the danger for

Piet to carry Hebrew papers back to Amersfoort, the rabbi said, "I will teach you seven Hebrew words, and I give you the authority—with my blessing—to be the one to officiate at the marriage of this couple. In the eyes of God they will be considered husband and wife."

The next day we saw Piet again. The look on his face told us that everything would work out for us. For a few moments after he arrived, he smoked heavily and looked around. Then he turned to us and said, "I have bad news and I have good news." We kept our eyes on his face, anxious to hear his next words. "I have thought over our situation, and I honestly believe that I, as a Catholic, am not qualified to marry you. Besides, the Hebrew words are all upside down in my head; I would marry you the wrong way. But," and now his face lit up, "the good news is that I tried again, and I did locate Mr. Van Dam. I talked to him, and he is willing to perform your wedding."

Felix's mother asked, "The synagogue—is it still open?"

Piet answered, "Nothing has happened there yet. I have to go home now, but I'll be back as soon as I can."

It was already the first week of July; time was running out for us. A deadline had been set by the Germans for Jewish people to leave the homes of Christians and be deported. This deadline was now looming large. Mr. Van Dam had been my Hebrew teacher, and he had told Piet, "For Flory, I will do the wedding, provided we will all be here yet."

When Piet came back later that day, he stressed that we had to act quickly. He had heard, via the resistance, that the Germans were making their final plans for the Jews.

There were certain laws in Holland regarding marriage. First, the couple had to take out a marriage license in the city hall and fill out the papers in the registrar's office. Next, documents of intention would be placed on the outside of the city hall building for fourteen days so people had time to inspect the paperwork. So technically, a Dutch couple had to wait at least two weeks before an official wedding could take place. In addition to this, I had another obstacle. I was underage and needed my mother's approval to marry, which meant that she too would be put in danger by coming along with us to city hall.

Piet calmed us down. He said, "You must set the date. I will then talk to the clerk at city hall. I know him well; he is a good, patriotic man. I will fix it so you won't have to wait fourteen days. In fact, I will fix everything. I promise that you will be able to go from city hall directly to the synagogue. I will confirm everything with Mr. Van Dam."

I told Piet that I was still concerned about a number of things, but he did not want to hear any of it. He said jokingly, "If there are no bombs falling on our heads, everything will be all right." Then he added, "Well, if we are bombed, at least we will have our names in the newspapers."

The date for our wedding was set for Thursday, July 9, 1942. I had always considered myself to be a romantic, and so, despite the strange circumstances of our pending wedding day, I still wanted to wear something white. I found an old white dress, on which I sewed some artificial flowers, which I took from a vase in the living room. I also found some old curtains, which in my mind would serve well as a veil. When I had completed my creation, I tried everything on to see what I looked like. It was pathetic. But with the help of those I loved, I still had good hopes for our future.

On the day of our wedding I had to wear my everyday clothes. I took a small suitcase in which I packed my improvised wedding dress along with my make-believe veil, and off we went. Felix had brought me a bouquet of lovely flowers, but for fear that they would draw too much attention from the Germans, I packed them instead in my suitcase.

Piet led the way to city hall, riding slowly on his bicycle ahead of us. Felix and I walked casually along the streets—our yellow stars prominently affixed to our clothing—as calmly as we could. Our mothers followed behind us, also wearing their stars. After quite a long walk we made it safely to city hall without being halted by a Nazi. The clerk, Mr. de Groot, was waiting for us. He was a wonderful man and saw to it that our registration went quickly and smoothly. He had all of the necessary documents ready. My mother signed the papers, and Felix's mother acted as a witness. We then received our family register booklet—without the royal seal and without our Dutch motto, Je Maintiendrai.

These first steps went well. We now had to head for the synagogue, which was quite a distance away. Again Piet rode his bike ahead of us. On the way to the synagogue we heard airplanes, but somehow we made it safely.

When we arrived at the temple, I was anxious to get out of my dress with the yellow star. I quickly changed my drab, everyday dress and put on my "wedding" dress. Felix put on a dark suit and a tie, and together we walked into the synagogue, where some friends and intermarried family members were waiting for us. My brother Ies and his wife, whom we had discovered were not yet in hiding, arrived a bit later.

Mr. Van Dam performed our wedding ceremony in a most dignified way, despite the crazy and unusual circumstances. He made the ceremony so beautiful that to this day his sermon is engraved in my heart. He began with a verse from the book of Ecclesiastes, as spoken by Koheleth, son of King David:

> Utter futility! All is futile!
> One generation goes, another comes, but the earth remains the same forever. There is a season for everything:
> A time for being born, and a time for dying
> A time for weeping and a time for laughing
> A time for reaping and a time for sowing.

Mr. Van Dam continued his beautiful oration, applying the sermon to the circumstances of our time. His conclusion touched me deeply. He pointed out that according to Jewish custom, upon the completion of any of the five books of the Torah, the entire congregation must recite the words, "Be strong, be strong, and let us strengthen one another, please God, give us strength." (In Aramaic, the words are Chazak, chazak ve 'nischazak.) Mr. Van Dam then explained that we were going through similar tribulations as those in the times the scriptures were written. He said when a person goes from one heartbreak to another, these words must be recited. And especially in a marriage, the words are recited twice so that one will give strength to the other.

Mr. Van Dam handed us the marriage certificate made out in Hebrew. After a warm embrace for me and a handshake for Felix, the ceremony was over. We were to be the last couple married in that lovely, two-hundred-year-old synagogue. Shortly after our wedding, Mr. and Mrs. Van Dam were deported to a concentration camp, never to return again. The synagogue was broken down by the Germans and used as a storage building during the war.

We had to return home. I quickly changed back into my old clothing and affixed the yellow star. We then began the long walk home accompanied by our family and friends. Nellie, Felix's sister, had graciously prepared some refreshments for us. The short, precious time we had together came quickly to an end.

The greatest gift and wonderful surprise on our wedding day was the arrival of my favorite cousin, Jacob de Haas of Rotterdam. He arrived without the yellow star on his clothes and without having mentioned to his parents that he was going to visit us in honor of our wedding. He took a terrible risk, and I shall never forget it. Jews still traveling by train or bus were required to show their papers to the conductor.

Piet had assured our families that he would immediately try to find hiding places for everyone. Felix and I, now husband and wife, hastily packed up some of the most necessary items to take with us to our hiding place. I had finally told my mother about the secret newspaper clippings I had collected and where I had hidden them. She told me that she had already given the Kolkmans a number of suitcases to keep for us, "just in case ..."

We said a tearful good-bye to our mothers and other family members, convinced that they too would find safe hiding places. I embraced my mother over and over. She seemed at peace knowing that we were in good hands with Piet.

At nightfall of this memorable day, we walked to our "honeymoon suite," a room in the attic of Piet's house, beginning another chapter of our journey through the Valley of Death.

CHAPTER 8

The Hiding Place

Three of four Brandsen girls: Nel, Henny, and Willie;
Bep, the youngest, is missing from this photograph.

Piet and Dina's house was a typical Dutch home: on the street
level was the sitting room, looking out to the backyard. The front
room—the best room—was reserved only for visitors or for Sunday
morning special occasions. Upstairs were several bedrooms, and above
those, on the next level, was the attic. This attic had two small rooms,
one of which was Opa's. There was only one toilet for the family, and
unfortunately, it was located way back in the yard, which as it would
turn out was a great handicap. There was a large kitchen parallel to
the sitting room. The kitchen door was open all the time.

Dina received us warmly. She said, "Make yourself at home while
I get the tea." All four children were staring at us as they sat around

the large table in the center of the kitchen. I believe that both Felix and I were very tense when we first arrived, but the warmth and the kindness of this family soon made us feel more at ease.

Piet confided completely in his wife and their four children because he began to speak freely about the resistance, how he would build hiding places, and ways that he would invent secret signs and codes in case strangers would come to visit.

This night Piet turned to Dina and exclaimed, "Dina, you must act casually. Do not change anything in your daily habits. I do not want the neighbors to become suspicious." To the children he admonished, "Just go ahead and play with your friends. Do everything that you always do, but do not utter a word to anyone about these two people who from now on will live with us." His stern look kept everyone in silence.

The children were to call us Uncle Jan and Aunt Marie; it turned out that they had family in Belgium by these names. Piet said to them, "Should anyone ever become suspicious or come to find something out, then these two people are your real aunt and uncle from Belgium." Soon the four girls were sent to bed. They were adorable, and in time I became quite fond of them. After the girls were asleep, Piet continued his conversation with us. He said in a reassuring and determined voice, "The first thing we must do is get you entirely new identity papers. I will contact my people in the resistance and explain everything." We nodded agreeably. We just sat there, not knowing what to expect in the home of total strangers.

Felix then asked, "Is there possibly any chance at all to escape over the border to Switzerland?"

Piet stopped smoking for a moment. He said, "Let me talk to someone whom I know well, and I will see what I can do."

It had become quite late, and Dina, getting up from the table, said, "Let's go upstairs. We all need a good night's sleep." Then turning to us with a smile, she continued, "We'll show you to your room."

A great surprise awaited us. Rather than having us stay in the attic, they insisted that we use their own spacious bedroom. Felix protested. "How can we accept this?" he said. "It is too much." But Piet explained, "Look here. In the attic you have to deal with Opa. In this room there is a balcony, so at least you can get some fresh air now and then." I'm sure he said this to make us feel better about using their room. We thanked them profusely, and as they left Dina gave me a big hug and said, "Pretty soon we will get rid of the *Rot-Moffen*."

Piet and Dina had warned us not to pay attention to Opa, the old man. They had told him that we were family members from far away in Belgium. In time, Opa referred to us as "the damned Belzen" because all too often he had to use the WC (water closet) back in the yard when one of us was using it. If we heard Dina talking to the neighbors at the same time, we knew we could not be seen going up to our room so we had to hold on firmly to a feeble lock in the door while Opa was on the other side cursing us, trying to get in.

Opa was in a very advanced stage of senility; none of the family members could carry on a conversation with him. I saw the girls occasionally going to his room to bring food. Sometimes he ate something while he was in the kitchen. Dina always had a large pot of soup or some other food on the stove, and so Opa could help himself whenever he was hungry or felt like eating. As time went by, Opa thought of an easier way to relieve himself. He used the chamber pot, then threw the pot with all its contents out of his attic room window. The pot—and the contents—always unfortunately landed on our balcony.

I had noticed a good number of religious figures in the house. Above our bed hung a large crucifix with the Christ figure attached to it. On a table in the corner of the bedroom stood a Madonna with child. Everything was so overwhelming for me that I cried most of the time, which was not a good thing for a new bride. I kept thinking of my mother and of Felix's family, but I would not dare burden Piet at that time with my deep sorrow.

The four girls were marvelous. I instinctively knew that we could trust them not to speak to anyone about us. Their parents had given them an excellent moral upbringing. We liked the girls from the beginning of our stay, and during those first two weeks we felt that they were fond of us too, especially Henny, who clung to me on every occasion that we saw each other. They never asked a thing, and there was never a hint on their part about the horrors that took place on the streets around them. They seemed to automatically understand the strong admonitions from their parents not to say a word to anyone about Felix and me. The girls were still on summer vacation from school and went about their typical days, spending lots of time with us upstairs in addition to doing chores and playing with friends. They really liked "Uncle Jan" and "Aunt Marie." For them it was a welcome change from the regular routine in their home. In the meantime, the war escalated and so did the horrors that the Germans inflicted on so many innocent people.

I missed my mother terribly, but Piet was constantly in touch with both of our families. He did, however, have to be very careful not to be seen too often in the Rubensstraat. Of course, Felix and I exchanged messages with our families via Piet, but these messages were never written. We could not put him in danger; we feared that a German would search him and find our notes.

Felix and I talked endlessly about escaping to Switzerland, wondering, on the one hand, if we could leave our mothers and, on the other hand, what dangers we would bring upon the Brandsen family if we stayed. It was tortuous to decide what to do.

We wanted to do something for Piet and his family, but it seemed as if nothing could possibly reciprocate their bravery. Nonetheless, we told them we'd do anything at all: help with housework, help the children with their schoolwork, sew, mend, whatever. It turned out that the most important issue in the household was that the two youngest girls needed help with their catechism lessons. I was only too happy to oblige.

Meanwhile, Dina adhered to her husband's admonition that she continue her usual routines, including talking with her neighbors at the front door of their home. These neighborly conversations sometimes lasted for an hour or more, and during that time there was no way for either of us to use the bathroom.

After a few weeks Piet told us that we would finally get to meet Moltjeveer, his friend from the resistance movement. He was to bring us new identity papers and discuss hiding places for my mother,

Felix's family, and Kurt. We would also discuss with him the possibility of escaping over the border to Switzerland.

That night after the children had gone to bed, the four of us sat around the kitchen table. A special knock on the door let Piet know that someone from the resistance movement was outside; it was Moltjeveer. Moltjeveer was his pseudonym; he was a very important leader in the resistance movement at the time and could not risk using his real name. He was a short, skinny man, about fifty years of age. His hair was grayish blond, and he wore glasses. When he spoke, it was evident that this man was intelligent and dedicated to his cause.

He handed us our new identity papers. We were fascinated with how authentic they looked. My photograph even captured the scar on my neck, a remnant of the tragedy of the SS *Simon Bolivar*. Moltjeveer said to us, "You must get to know your new names and all of the details contained in these papers." Felix was now "Jan Van Ophuizen," and I was now "Hendrika Helmina Geijtenbeek." The papers also included false birthdates and addresses and were stamped properly, including the words *valid for five years*. The papers also read, MISUSE IS PUNISHABLE!

It was amazing to us what the resistance movement could accomplish. We thanked both Moltjeveer and Piet profusely, realizing what danger the acts placed them in. Our conversation then turned to hiding places for our families and the possibility of crossing the border. Moltjeveer said to us, "There definitely is a possibility that people could be smuggled from Belgium to France, then escape into Switzerland. But it is a dangerous undertaking. If you want to take the risk, you must make up your mind quickly and let me know tomorrow night. I will contact our most reliable people. I'll return here tomorrow night at the same time." Felix looked at me, and I at him. Then the four of us talked until quite late.

Back in our room, Felix and I weighed the pros and cons of escaping. Felix said, "I have a feeling the war will last much longer than we originally thought. How can we impose on these brave people? It might take years." I agreed that we did not want to jeopardize their lives and the lives of their children. Food was becoming scarce, and there was the possibility that someone might betray us and turn us in to the Nazis. Our thoughts were wild and confused.

Finally, we decided to leave, and early the next morning we told Piet we would try to cross the border. Although we saw a look of shock on his face, his voice remained calm, and he said he would contact Moltjeveer. With his hand on the doorknob as he left our room, he turned to us and said, "As far as Dina and I are concerned, you can stay here with us as long as the war is on." We were deeply touched but resolved in our decision.

Later that day Piet came back to our room and said to us, "I told Moltjeveer of your decision; it is now in the hands of the resistance movement. Since time is of the essence, you must be ready to leave in a few days. Pack up only the most necessary items; be sure you have your new identity papers."

Felix and I looked at each other, our hearts pounding. I could not eat a thing that day, nor could I sleep that night.

Finally the evening of our escape arrived. Someone from the resistance movement was to come for us and take us to a certain place, where again, others in the movement would guide us over the Dutch border. We were not told anything further than this; we were not to know or question anything more. The children had not been told about our leaving. Dina had made tea and was serving it in the front room, where the four of us were sitting in large chairs waiting for the knock on the door that would signal the beginning of what would certainly be a perilous journey. Piet, as always, was smoking and appeared to be in deep concentration.

Not a word was spoken, until at last Felix and I broke the silence by thanking them again for all they had done for us. I said, "Give the girls a big hug for us." Piet nodded; Dina's hand shook, the teacup rattling.

It was one of those evenings, similar to many in the past, where my emotions—anxiety, tension, foreboding—were magnified. I felt my heart beating fast, but I kept up my outwardly calm demeanor. Felix held tight to a small travel bag in which he had packed some toilet articles and shaving supplies. Whatever money we had was also in the bag.

In the corner of the room was a large grandfather's clock, which pealed a loud clang every fifteen minutes. Paintings and religious figures in the room shook each time the clock let out its horrendous clang. It was a warm summer evening with no breeze. The clock tracking every moment, the ominous silence, the stillness in the air created an eeriness that I can still feel. I vividly remember the far-off sound of people talking in the street, a dog barking, and watching Dina mend some of the children's clothes. The waiting became almost unbearable, so much so that the loud clang of the clock seemed to pierce my eardrums every minute rather than every fifteen minutes.

At ten o'clock that night, just to break the silence, I said to Piet, "Isn't it becoming too late to go over the border?" He removed the pipe from his mouth and simply shook his head.

Finally, at about eleven-thirty, the special knock was heard. Piet answered the door, and there stood Moltjeveer, his face drawn and pale. We immediately knew something was wrong. Moltjeveer sat down and told us the awful news: a carefully planned transport of seven Jewish people over the border had been discovered by the Nazis, and all seven of them were shot. This tragedy left us in a state of shock; for more than an hour no one could utter a word. At some point during that hour Moltjeveer left; we were so devastated we did not even see him leave. Finally, Felix and I went upstairs to our room. Over and over in my mind I repeated the words of Mr. Van Dam, "Be strong, be strong, and let us strengthen one another, please God, give us strength."

+>==<+

Luckily, Piet and Dina had not said anything about our planned departure to the children. The next morning began the same as it had two weeks before, we on our guard every minute, desperately trying not to be seen or heard.

Since it was too dangerous to eat our meals downstairs where neighbors might see us, the girls always brought something to our room for us to eat. Later in the evenings we could go downstairs because the kitchen was then locked and the curtains drawn. During these evenings Felix mostly talked to Piet about the war, the Germans, the Jewish people, and the hiding places for my mother and for Felix's family. I helped Dina in the kitchen, and afterward, when the four girls went to bed, we made tea. It all sounds like a peaceful existence, but our minds were full of anguish. If we could only know for sure that our families would be hidden somewhere, our situation would perhaps be easier for us to bear.

Moltjeveer and Piet were desperately trying to find sympathetic people who were willing to take the risk of hiding Jews. We heard through Piet that a great number of Jewish couples, as well as small children and babies, had been picked up by the Nazis. Their homes had been sealed, and they were sent to Camp Westerbork, from where they were immediately transported.

Through Piet, we were still in touch with my mother and Felix's family. I yearned to see my mother, but it could not be. Piet told us that my brother's store had been sealed up, and Piet was not able to find his whereabouts. It was simply too dangerous for Piet to be seen so much in town trying to find out information.

Felix started keeping a diary, which, of course, he hid upstairs very carefully. Piet also had a crystal (radio) so well hidden that even a clever German would not be able to find it. We knew from the BBC how the war was progressing, where the English armies were, what the Americans did, about the meetings between Churchill and Roosevelt, and especially how the Russians courageously fought against the Germans.

The Germans had now established several more concentration camps in Holland. There was one in Vught (a small city in the province of NoordBrabant, in the south); another one in Putten, to the north; and of course the one in Amersfoort, where my Uncle Isse van Zuiden had been killed. The camp in Amersfoort turned out to be one of the most vicious. Through the resistance, we heard that the Germans were slaughtering people on a daily basis there.

It was now eight months since January 1942, the month when the Germans announced that Holland would soon be *Judenrein*, cleansed of Jews. Already Jews had been forcibly removed from a great number of cities: Zaandam, Arnhem, Hilversum. The next target would be Amersfoort. We were all in great despair. The Germans now had the addresses of all Dutch Jews. At night they came to town, and by the next morning many Jews had been deported, forced to leave all of their belongings behind.

We learned through Piet that my beloved Aunt Flora and Uncle Jules Frank, who had so graciously received Felix's family, were still in their home in the Joannes van Dieststraat.

The deadline for the deportations neared. On Sunday, August 16, 1942, an order appeared in all newspapers by the German authorities commanding that all Jews between the ages of sixteen and forty be deported to Germany, and on Friday night, August 21, everyone over the age of forty would be picked up by the German police. Everyone was "allowed" to take his or her valuables, carefully packed according to Nazi-style instructions.

The Nazis also applied their rules to Jews who had converted to another religion and even to people who were mentally disabled. Seven hundred Roman Catholics of Jewish descent also had been taken away. This was clearly revenge by the Germans, the result of a telegram sent to Seyss-Inquart by the Catholic churches in protest of the deportation of Jews.

We later learned from the resistance that among several Carmelite nuns in a convent in Limburg, in the south of Holland, was a woman named Edith Stein, born of Orthodox Jewish parents. Edith converted to Catholicism, and during the war she was dragged to Camp Westerbork and then deported to Auschwitz. When the public tried to help her, she was quoted as saying, "Please don't bother for me; others need help more than I do." Edith Stein was canonized by the Catholic Church in 1998.

Around this same time telegrams were sent to all police stations stating that every day from midnight until two o'clock in the morning extra trains would be running to transport Jews to Germany, and from there to the death camps.

My mother still lived with the Kolkmans in the Rubensstraat. I had become so anxious that I could not eat or sleep. Adding to this stress was the fact that I did not want to show how anxious I was, not even to Felix. I did not want to become a burden to anyone. I was quite thin when I got married; by this time I looked emaciated. Piet, noticing how thin I had become, said, "Please don't feel shy; we have enough to eat, and you must eat to keep healthy and strong." But the possible fate of my mother and other loved ones was constantly on my mind and eroded whatever strength I had.

One day toward the end of August, Moltjeveer came to Piet's house and told us that he had found a hiding place for my mother. He gave the address to Piet, who would go to pick up my mother that night. I was elated. The evening came, and with great anxiety we waited for Piet to return with good news about my mother. But when he finally arrived, we could immediately see that something was very wrong. He removed the pipe from his mouth and said, "Let's sit down. I have bad news." Turning to me he continued, "Your mother is away. I have inquired and learned that those filthy Nazis put many people on the train to Westerbork, including your mother."

Although I heard his voice explaining more, everything became a blur to me. I was incapable of hearing or understanding another word. My mother, the love of my life, in the hands of the Nazis. What would they do to her? What was her fate? Could I go on living not knowing where or how she was now? My angel mother, who would not even kill a fly. So attentive, modest, shy, soft-spoken, kind, and loving; my mother in the hands of those barbarians. It was inconceivable to me.

Piet was talking, but his voice sounded distant, obscured. I vaguely heard him say something about obtaining a medical testimonial from a local doctor stating that my mother was sick and under a physician's care and not fit to travel on a transport. What had happened, I heard Piet say, was that the remainder of the Jewish community in Amersfoort had planned a last prayer meeting in the synagogue to bid farewell to their beloved country and to commemorate the upcoming festival of the Jewish New Year, Rosh Hashanah, which that year fell on the first days of September. My mother had left her home to attend but was picked up by the Germans. Several weeks later we received a farewell letter from my mother. She had apparently thrown it from the train. Kind people—people we will never know—mailed it to us. Every year I light a candle for my mother on the Jewish High Holy Days.

Piet's language was always very colorful. Cursing the Germans, he came over to where I was sitting. He had a strong drink in his hand, and he said, "I will take the first train to Westerbork tomorrow morning. I'll have the doctor's letter with me, and I will do everything in my power to get your mother out."

I know at the time I was in such shock over my mother's fate that most of what he said was a blur to me. I looked over at Felix and noticed how pale and drawn his face was. He said to me, "This is the greatest tragedy in the history of mankind. Germany was such a cultured nation with the finest universities; it produced famous writers, composers, painters ... you name it. How can it be that people with doctorate degrees, people who are generally so intelligent, have turned into murderers? How can they commit such brutal crimes without thinking twice about what they're doing?"

For several moments we sat in awkward silence, unable to find the strength to move. Felix continued, "What can be done about Flory's mother? What will become of my mother and Nel and Kurt? What is their fate going to be?"

Dina served the hot tea. She said, "Drink your tea and let's get some rest. Everything is in the hands of God. We must trust in him." She then made the sign of the cross. Piet did the same. Felix and I went up to our room.

Later that night I searched for the sermon that Mr. Van Dam had given us on our wedding day. I held on to it because I drew comfort from the words. I found the sermon in my purse and read and reread the words from the book of Ecclesiastes, which Mr. Van Dam had so eloquently recited at our wedding. Among the verses I read: "God brings everything to pass precisely at its time. There is a time for war, and a time for peace, a time for loving and a time for hating ..." That night, however, as I lay in bed, I could not find any solace in those words. I preferred to focus on "a time for hating." I hated the Germans, and I promised myself that I would never set foot in Germany should we survive. I knew then that the feeling of hate would be with me forever. I spent the rest of the night writing a long letter to my mother, telling her how much I loved her and how I hoped that we would soon be reunited.

Felix and I had a sleepless night. Very early the next morning Piet knocked on our door to tell us he was off to catch the train to Westerbork. I gave him the letter I had written to my mother, which he hid in his shoe. He had to be very careful. After our daily routine of washing, getting dressed, sneaking out to the WC, and having something to eat, the front door opened. We could not believe our eyes; Piet had returned. Although we were used to the unexpected, this time we were overcome with fear. Dina and even the children came to our room with Piet; they were all anxious to hear what had happened. Piet told us that there had been a train derailment caused by the resistance. In retaliation, the Germans had lined up civilians and shot them. These were the common actions of people who considered themselves part of the "master race."

We begged Piet to stay home and not try to go to Westerbork again; we feared putting his family in danger. He agreed but said that he would try again the next day to catch a train to the camp and deliver the doctor's letter. In the course of the day, as we sat in our room, we heard all kinds of commotion: people from the resistance movement coming in and out of the house, talking excitedly.

The next day Piet did go to Westerbork. It was a long day for us, as every day had been, but on this day we were especially anxious. That night Piet returned safe and sound. But the expression on his face told us that my mother's fate had been sealed. Piet learned that she had been put on a transport in the direction of Poland.

About one week later during the morning hours, I suddenly heard my mother's voice calling my name. It was so clear that I even turned around, as if I would find her standing there behind me. In my heart I knew that it was the moment she died.

It was the end of the second week of September 1942.

LETTER FROM MY MOTHER

September 7, 1942

My very beloved children:

This is my farewell letter to you my dear children.

I was unexpectedly taken away Friday night by the German SS and driven in a police car to Amsterdam.

We had to walk in Amsterdam from "Het Westeinde" to "Het Meyerplein," which took us one and one-half hour. I was wearing a thin dress; they did not give me time. I have no money on me, no hat and I miss my glasses.

From Amsterdam we were transported in a freight car to Hooghalen, where we had to walk for two hours at two o'clock in the night, to Camp Westerbork.

Every half-hour large transports from Amsterdam arrive here. Among the people are poor wretches, some of the sick and bewildered, in their eighties. My heart is heavy. I cannot describe the misery that is going on here.

I am very nervous; it is cold and dirty here and there is no way to sleep. We have not had anything to eat since I was deported.

I feel that this will be my last journey; we know what the Germans have in mind for us. We were told that we have to go again on a transport but I don't know where to.

If there is anything left in our home in Rotterdam, maybe the furniture and other household effects can be sold and the proceeds will be for you, my beloved children.

I am sure that God will save you all.

I kiss and embrace you all many, many times. If it is God's will maybe we will see each other again.

Your faithful and loving mother

I translated this letter from Dutch. It was written and thrown from a train by my mother, Alijda Cohen-Van Beek.

CHAPTER 9

Fear, Our Companion

My mother

I don't know how I was able to get through the several days following my mother's deportation. I lay on the bed most days trying to trace the moments before her disappearance, minute by minute. What was she feeling? What was she thinking? What would she have said to me? I thought constantly about what she must have gone through. Felix, Piet, and Dina did their best to console me, but my heart was broken. A piece of my soul had left with my mother, with whom I had been so very close.

None of us was able to predict how long the dreadful war would last. I often felt that I would not be able to survive. Too many despicable events had taken place, one after the other. The worst thing was that I believed I could not openly show my grief and become a burden to the brave people who gave us protection and shelter under the most dangerous of circumstances.

One day during the third week in September we received bad news again. Felix's mother had become ill, and she needed an operation. One of her neighbors had taken her to the local hospital, which at that time was forbidden. The Germans did not allow Jews to be treated in the hospitals.

Piet came to our room that morning with the news. He sat down on the bed, waiting for us to calm down. Finally, he said, "You know, if the operation is behind us, the situation for now might be good. She is safe in the hospital, and she must stay there as long as she is recuperating. I will contact one of my friends to ensure that she is okay."

Felix and I were devastated. Each time there was another problem to solve, and we were powerless to do anything. Felix asked Piet questions about Nel and Kurt's future; Piet answered, with a concerned yet confident tone, "I must find a hiding place for your sister and Kurt, but they will have to get married first."

I kept thinking, "What a struggle to stay alive ... Is it all worth it?"

Before Piet left our room he stood up and said, "I'll come up with something if it's the last thing I do." Then turning to me, he said, "And you, young lady, take it easy. Eventually we will get rid of the *Rot-Moffen*." This became a slogan, and it helped everyone mentally.

When evening came Piet called for us to come downstairs. Turning to Felix he said, "I know a family down the street. They are a middle-aged couple, good patriots, and very religious *gereformeerd* [translated from the Dutch, Calvinists]. I have a feeling that if I go there and speak to them, they might want to help."

Felix said, "Are you sure that it would be safe to let them know that we are here?"

"I am convinced," Piet answered. "We have to take that gamble, anyway." The conversation continued, and Piet said, "I will go there tomorrow morning and ask them if they can take your sister and Kurt for a short time, until I have found a permanent place for them."

All of us were engrossed in our own thoughts. Finally Felix said, "I see no other way but to go ahead and ask them. All of our lives are hanging by a thin thread anyway. But, Piet, I don't want you in any danger on account of us."

I understood better now why so many Jewish families had taken their own lives and the lives of their children rather than falling prey to the Germans and facing such slow, morbid destruction. It was because of Piet and Dina that we did not give up. Their courage was unbelievable, their demeanor gallant.

At night in bed, Felix and I talked about everything for a long time. He said, "All we can do is pray." I kept looking at the Madonna on the table in our room. Her face reminded me somehow of my mother. It represented serenity, innocence, tranquillity. I don't know what came over me, but I was glad that the statue was there.

The next morning around noon, Piet came to our room. His face was glowing. "I talked to the Van den Hoevens," he began. "I explained the situation as it is now; then I asked them if they could help to save a young Jewish couple." Piet stopped smoking and then continued. "They were a bit reluctant at first, but they are very religious and they understood that lives have to be saved."

We asked him a few questions about this couple. It turned out that the Van den Hoevens had four adult children, and they were devout Calvinists. They told Piet that they would speak with their children, who were all old enough to understand the severity of the issue and the importance of keeping this a secret. Finally, after a lengthy conversation, Piet stood up, took his pipe in his hand, and said, "I'm going to see Nel and Kurt, and I will also find out how your mother is doing."

After he left us, our tension was high. "We must do something to occupy ourselves," Felix said. "It is not good to just sit here the whole day. Maybe we can help Piet or do something with the children." I agreed, but first I had to calm myself; I first needed to know what would happen with Felix's mother and with Nel and Kurt.

That night we went downstairs again after the doors and the curtains were closed. The house was very quiet. The children's vacation was over, and they had returned to school. On this evening they were already in bed. Dina was preparing tea, and Piet was smoking. Piet looked pensive. We prepared ourselves for yet another phase in this saga of horror and sadness. Decisions were about to be made to save—or lose—three more lives.

Looking at Felix, Piet began: "First of all, your mother is safe in the hospital. The operation went well. They promised to keep her there until it is safe to get her out." I heard Felix utter a sigh of relief, knowing that for the time being, his mother was all right. Piet took a sip of his tea and continued, "I spoke with Nel and Kurt, and they agreed to get married. They realize that the time for pro-crastination is over and that they have to seize the moment for the chance to go into hiding." He added, "And remember, I still have the authorization from Rabbi Tal!"

As we sipped our tea, no one spoke for a while. Piet continued by emphasizing how serious things were. He said, "I am now deeply involved with the resistance. We have contact with England, and I have immediate access to all important information. The *Einsatz-gruppen* are all over in our country and all other occupied coun-tries." *Einsatzgruppen* translated from the German means "troops," and it specifically applies to those troops designed and trained to kill, such as the SS, the SD, and the Gestapo.

Though I knew by now that the Nazis could kill almost non-chalantly, I shuddered. Going into more explicit detail, Piet contin-ued, "A number of resistance people, as well as innocent citizens, have been killed. The *Rot-Moffen* will soon organize the last roundup of Jews: the old, the sick, the very young, and the babies. All who in their eyes are undesirable elements must be wiped out."

It felt like such a long evening. Piet had turned on the crys-tal—after he had locked all of the doors and made sure the cur-tains were drawn. We all listened to the BBC and especially what the commentators in England had to say about the development of the war. We knew that it had previously been a bitter winter in Russia and that the German troops had been forced back into de-fensive positions near Stalingrad.

Felix, who was so well informed about many details of history, spoke: "If Stalingrad can hold out and drive the Germans back, then, in my estimation, the Germans will lose the war eventually. How much longer it will last, we don't know. And how many lives it will cost, who knows."

There was no access to sleeping pills during those days. I spent the vast majority of nights wide awake. Often, both of us had bad nightmares, which interrupted what little sleep we did get. I frequently reached for Mr. Van Dam's wedding sermon, which I had carefully hidden underneath the bed. I tried to make sense of what was happening, but I always ended up with feelings of anger, doubt, uncertainty, and, above all, hatred for the Germans.

Now events began to take place quickly, one after the other. We learned from Piet, through his secret connections, that the German police had invaded several Jewish homes to "take inventory," whereby the Jewish families had to fill out lengthy statements regarding their household effects, valuables, rent or mortgage payments, and other details. After they were questioned, they were arrested because, according to the Germans, they were not supposed to be living where they were anymore, anyway.

The few remaining Jewish families had gone to the synagogue—what was left of it—and blown the shofar (the ram's horn) to usher in the Jewish New Year 5703. We understood that shortly after our wedding the four Holy Scrolls (the Torahs) had been removed from the temple by some of the synagogue members and brought to safety in an undisclosed hiding place.

During this same week Piet told us that Nel and Kurt were married at the home in the Rubensstraat 23; Piet and one of the remaining Jewish members of the temple officiated. The next morning around noon Piet came to our room to bring us the latest news about Felix's mother. He told us that someone from the resistance had talked to one of the doctors in the hospital, and arrangements had been made to pick up his mother on a certain evening during the third week of September. She too would go into hiding. Piet informed us that the same night that he checked on Felix's mother, Nel and Kurt had been safely escorted to the Van den Hoeven family home; they had left everything behind in the Rubensstraat.

In spite of the time he spent in the resistance and at work, Piet managed to build a small hiding place in our room underneath the staircase. I prayed we would never be forced to use it. Piet told us of his plans to build more hiding places downstairs in case someone who was not involved with the resistance—and not sympathetic to the cause—should come into the house unexpectedly. He talked about eventually building an air raid shelter in the yard since there were more and more air raids as the war escalated.

A few days passed when Piet told us that his trip to Rotterdam was set for the next morning. He had also set a date with the hospital to pick up Felix's mother. For the time being, until a more permanent hiding place could be found, she too would stay with the Van den Hoevens.

Piet left early the next morning, letting us know that he would be back in the afternoon and that he would definitely inquire about my family while he was in Rotterdam. At around three o'clock in the afternoon that day we heard Piet's voice. He immediately ran into our room; he looked absolutely stunned. He said, "Jan, I found your mother on the street. I took her to the Van den Hoevens." Dina also ran up to our room. All of us were flabbergasted.

What had happened, we learned, was that there was an unexpected razzia by the Germans at the hospital. The doctors and hospital staff—thinking they would save Felix's mother's life—let her go into the streets.

Piet, on his way home from Rotterdam, decided to take a different route home from the railroad station than he usually took. He could not explain his reasons why; it was more impulse than anything else. Although he had gone his familiar way home from the railroad station hundreds of times, on this particular day something prompted him to try another route. On his way home he came upon an elderly woman who had a familiar face. It was, of course, Felix's mother. She was sitting on the curb, crying and praying that she would find help. She had wandered, pushing her frail body for blocks, not knowing where to go or what to do. She was still weak from her operation.

Piet immediately took her away from the main streets and brought her to the Van den Hoevens. If ever a true miracle happened, it was on this day. It could not be explained any other way than a guardian angel watching over her.

After Piet told us the details, we stood there silent for quite some time. Finally Piet said, "You two must take in some fresh air. Take some deep breaths." He opened the door to the small balcony, and as I counted my breaths—one, two, three, inhale—I sensed that the three of us were also trying to breathe in some understanding of the magnitude of what had taken place that day.

Piet broke the silence by lighting another cigarette. He said, "I have to rush off again, but I'll see you tonight, downstairs. I have some new information for you, Marietje. In the meantime, try to relax."

I interrupted him, "But, Piet, can't you tell me now?" But he insisted that we would talk later, after he returned.

When evening came Dina called us to come downstairs. We sat around the table, as usual, Dina busy with preparing and serving a surrogate tea. (Everything edible on the market after German occupation was "surrogate": tea, coffee, bread, etc. because the Germans sent the good products to Germany, to their own people. We ate sugar beets and tulip bulbs in place of onions. Some people even ate cats, which were called "roof rabbits"). Piet sat in his lazy chair, smoking. Piet began, "We have to be grateful that your mother is safe, Jan. But now I have some bad news for you, Marietje." Piet continued, "I went to the address you gave me of your Aunt and Uncle de Haas; no one was there. I then inquired at a neighbor's home. They told me that your family had received the summons to go to the train station to be relocated—well, you know, as the Germans call it. It sounds better than openly saying 'to send them to the death camps.' The neighbors were adamant to help your family find hiding places, but your uncle refused to bother anyone or to be the cause of their deaths, so he went voluntarily to the train station. He had said good-bye to his family, neighbors, and friends."

As Piet spoke, I began to think that it would have been better if we had drowned in the North Sea; we would have been spared this endless heartache. We had no choice now but to deal as best we could with these awful circumstances.

I asked Piet, "What happened to my Aunt Sien and my cousin Jaap?"

No one knew their whereabouts, Piet told me; the neighbors hoped they were hiding somewhere. Piet added, I believe to console us, "I know that your aunt and uncle in the Van Dieststraat are still okay. I have my connections; they will keep me up-to-date."

Later, upstairs in our room, Felix and I said to each other, "What next?" I was unable to fall asleep, and I became engrossed in my thoughts. I thought, "Every second of time that passes will never come back; each moment is gone forever. How will the next moments be? Will we be dead or alive? All of us are just a second in history."

CHAPTER 10

Working for the Resistance

Jewish identification papers issued by the Germans

There was no way we could be in direct contact with Felix's family, nor could Piet be seen at the Van den Hoevens'; it would have provoked suspicion. Piet said to us that he would drop by the Van den Hoeven home on occasion during the evenings so it would look like a casual visit. The Van den Hoevens, fearing serious repercussions, hinted that they did not want much contact with Piet since they had three Jewish people hiding in their home.

The resistance had also found a hiding place for Kurt's mother. She was with an older couple somewhere near a small town called Baarn. Felix was worried about how Kurt's mother would manage without knowing a word of Dutch. Piet joked, "Well, it might be

a good thing because now she cannot get into trouble with them!"
I had met Kurt's mother on only a few occasions. She seemed to
be a friendly elderly woman. We knew she was a diabetic, and our
concern was how she would manage without any medication.

None of us knew, from a medical perspective, how serious her
condition was. We heard from time to time that she was doing all
right. Perhaps the fact that there was not enough food available
automatically kept her on a diet; this may have stabilized her illness. She lived through the war, but unfortunately, a few months
after the liberation, she passed away.

One evening Piet said to us, "I was at the Van den Hoevens';
everyone is okay, and I have a message for both of you from your
mother. Your family wishes you a Happy New Year, and your mother
wants you to observe the Atonement Day [the Yom Kippur High
Holy Day]. She said it is around this time."

I became upset and angry. Although I tried to keep my anger
under control, I blurted out, "What should we atone for! God should
atone for what he does to his people! I won't hear about it, and I have
no message back."

An awkward silence filled the air. An air raid siren began to blare,
and we heard planes flying low overhead. After a long, tense few minutes, the all-clear signal blew, and, much to my relief, the High Holy
Day conversation was over. It was not mentioned again that evening.
I intended to be a good and dedicated wife to Felix, but the circumstances under which we found ourselves did not allow this.

I had mentioned to Piet that I knew how to type, a skill I had
learned at the practical language school in Rotterdam. Piet was elated

to hear this and said he would mention it to *Het Parool*, the newspaper of the resistance movement and one of the most important underground newspapers during the war years. *Het Parool* was secretly distributed among the most trustworthy and patriotic citizens. The newspaper contained, among other things, the latest news from the BBC, information on the Germans' current strategies, and crimes the Nazis committed against the Dutch people.

The winter had already set in, and food became even more scarce. Piet had indicated that the resistance was very busy with falsifying food coupons. One evening he said to us, "If Marietje can type, it would be a big help. We have lists of people who are hiding Jewish people; they urgently need extra coupons; we also help families of the resistance workers." I was more than happy to help; Felix said he would take the administration of this project on himself. Piet said, "I am going to speak with the people from *Het Parool*. They will not betray me for hiding Jewish people in my home."

While I was glad to be of assistance, I had this strange feeling that a calamity would befall us again. I talked to Felix about it, but he explained, as was his philosophy, that we were branded anyway so we might as well make ourselves useful in any way we could. I agreed with him, but I felt uncomfortable that people would know where we were. Of course I was also concerned about the safety of the Brandsen family.

In the winter of 1942 Felix began to feel deep pain in his shoulder and arm. He could not sleep at night, and yet he could not visit a doctor for his condition. At first Felix did not want to mention his discomfort to Dina and Piet. However, as intuitive as Piet was, he began to sense that something was wrong. Finally, Felix told them of his pain. Dina said, "I know of a remedy; it is an old Dutch recipe and it always helps. Believe it or not, it is petroleum."

In order to get some petroleum, Piet had to lie and say that it was he who had the pain in his shoulder and arm. In those days one had to think through everything—and every lie—to protect oneself. Shortly thereafter, Piet came home with a container of petroleum, and Felix started his treatment immediately. Within a week, the pains disappeared. Needless to say, the treatment smelled awful. Even Opa mumbled about the odor and accused the "darned Belzen" of bringing gasoline into the house.

Piet, Dina, Felix, and I listened every day to the forbidden crystal. Before we turned it on, we had to lock all the doors and be sure that not a bit of light shone through the windows to the outside of the house. The Germans were known to shoot into homes that did not completely follow the rules of the blackout times.

We closely followed the battle of Stalingrad; this was, for us, the turning point. The Germans had already survived a horribly cold winter in Russia, and another winter was approaching. Our anxiety worked overtime as the tension grew; we did not want to see the Germans gain control of Russian oil fields, which were located in Siberia and in the Caucasian Mountains. The war seemed to go on forever.

As we were waiting to see if we could help and work for the resistance, Felix and I made ourselves as useful as possible. We had to be extremely careful not to make any noise; we were constantly on our guard because during the day we could hear people coming in and out of the house.

The girls were wonderful. Even though they always brought playmates home, they instinctively knew what to do and what not to do, with us hiding upstairs. Meanwhile, winter deepened. The days were short, and darkness fell in the afternoon. When the children's playmates left, the girls came upstairs, where I helped them with their homework and catechism or played games with them. After they had gone to bed I helped Dina with sewing and mending.

During the days Felix worked on his diary or he polished shoes. At night he listened to the tiny crystal with Piet; afterward they often had a lengthy conversation about the war. The days were difficult for us. I prayed a lot during those days. I prayed that we would not be discovered and that no harm would befall the Brandsen family on account of our being there. I prayed that we would not get sick. But mostly I prayed for my mother that a miracle would happen and we would be reunited again. We hadn't the faintest idea where my siblings were. Because I could not fathom a God who would allow the Jewish people to be annihilated, I prayed to no one in particular. I simply addressed my prayers "to whom it may concern," which included God in any case.

+>==<+

Piet stayed busy building hiding places. He was working on another one downstairs in the hallway near the kitchen, in a room that had been a storage area that most Dutch homes were equipped with. As was the custom in Holland, people used these spaces for preserving vegetables and other homemade foods. Building a hiding place here was a brilliant idea because one could quickly enter it from the right or the left. Coming from the yard or the kitchen, we could disappear into this hiding place from one direction should a neighbor come to the front door. If we were on the staircase and the doorbell rang, then we could enter the hiding place from the other. Piet had also made a double door for this hideout; it was larger than the one in our bedroom upstairs. Both hiding places were frightening; we could hardly stand being in either one since little air could come in from the outside.

Piet was also busy making an electrical connection leading from the front entrance of the home to our room. In case of danger, someone could push a button downstairs and a red light would go on in our room, indicating that we must immediately hide. By the end of October Piet had completed all of these security measures.

In the meantime we kept ourselves as busy as possible. We were working on a dollhouse for the children with what little material was available. It was a tedious job, but seeing the joy on the girls' faces and the enthusiasm with which they ran up to our room after school each day was the greatest reward we could ask for.

One evening Piet came home with a suitcase in which he had hidden a typewriter. He turned to me and said, "Marietje, I'll bring it upstairs and then you can try it out. But one of the *Parool* people wants to come and make sure that all hiding places are in order, insisting that we have a rehearsal of what to do in case of an emergency before we start working for them. I will be honest with you— there is danger connected to the work here."

Danger was no stranger to us; we always felt as if our lives were in peril. Felix was marvelous in this respect. He said to Piet, "One way or the other, I will fight till death, and whatever I can do for the cause, I will. It is an honor to participate."

The next evening after the children had gone to bed, the four of us went upstairs to our room to practice. The plan was for Piet to push the button that was connected to the light in our room. As soon as we saw the red light go on, we were to quickly and very quietly sneak into our hiding place. The red light appeared, and in we went. Piet had done a superb job. With great ingenuity, he had designed a lock on the inside of the small compartment in our room; he had also made a second door so that the entrance had double doors. We executed the practice exactly as planned, but once inside the compartment I was struck by a terrible attack of claustrophobia. I could not wait to get out. What would happen if we really had to hide this way?

Late one evening a person from the resistance came to Piet's home. He brought with him a small suitcase filled with lists of names, food coupons, documents, and papers from *Het Parool*. This man did not mince words. He said, "I am Jeroen." It was not his real name, of course. He shook hands with us, then continued, "I want to see the layout and the safety devices." First, we all went upstairs while Piet was explaining the details of our emergency plan. Jeroen then said to Piet, "She must not type while you have people downstairs. No sound must be heard, ever." After Jeroen inspected our hiding place upstairs, we went downstairs so he could see the other hiding place. In this one we were able to stand up while inside.

Dina, always hospitable, offered us all some tea. Jeroen thanked her politely but declined. He preferred to spend time discussing more details. He admonished us to keep the secret papers in the hiding place as much as possible and to only take out the lists that needed to be typed. Felix was to do all of the administration, and Piet would be in direct contact with the resistance as far as our work was concerned. Jeroen stayed for a while longer, asking about the children, the neighbors, Opa, and any visitors. After he left we carefully closed all doors and made sure all were locked up. Then we went to bed.

The next morning we started to work on the assignment. I could type pretty quickly, but all the while I had to listen for people downstairs. If so, I had to stop typing immediately; I always had to be on guard.

The food coupons were masterly counterfeited. They were distributed to families who had people in hiding, to families of the resistance workers, and to all who needed food, which was scarce. Our assignment was to make lists with the names of people who needed to receive the coupons: how many were to be given out, the names of the people, dates. The coupons had to be numbered so that accurate records could be kept. Piet was responsible for the distribution of these coupons. We also had to keep records of documents and type duplicates of information, as well as articles for *Het Parool*.

We soon got the hang of it, and the days went by a bit more quickly. On Sundays the whole family went to church, leaving Felix and me alone with Opa. We always carefully locked all of the doors and hoped that Opa would not have to go to the WC and, therefore, unlock the kitchen door.

Christmas came and went, and as the year 1943 began, the war raced on. Now the Americans were deeply involved. One evening in the first week of February, while Dina and I were mending socks and the two men were listening to the crystal, Piet and Felix suddenly began to shout jubilantly. A Russian general had surrounded Hitler's sixth army and destroyed it. The German General von Paulus surrendered, and the Germans were driven out. Piet and Felix believed this was the turning point of Hitler's war.

There was also bad news: our dear friend Kolkman had been shot and killed by the Nazis during a sabotage attempt by the resistance workers, which he was a part of. He was only in his mid-thirties; all of us were deeply saddened by this terrible news, and we hoped that his wife and two children would be able to cope with the loss.

One night not long after this, Felix developed a terrible toothache. At first we gave him aspirin, but as the days wore on, the toothache grew worse. He was clearly in agony, and we could see how much he suffered; at times he was even doubled over in pain. Piet and Dina realized that professional help was needed. Piet said, "I know a physician who is connected with the resistance. I'll ask Jeroen if I can talk to him."

The next day an arrangement was made, and Piet went to see the doctor. When he returned home, he came to our room and said, "There is no other way but to go and see a dentist. The doctor explained to me that the problem may develop into an infection; he cannot do anything about it." Turning to Felix, Piet added, "My friends in the resistance will find a good, patriotic dentist whom we can trust." The same evening Jeroen came to the house with the name of a reliable dentist, who, unfortunately, lived quite far from

Piet's home. We had a decision to make: take the chance of Felix becoming very sick or take the risk of going to this dentist. We decided that the latter was better.

So one evening, after all had been arranged for us, the three of us—Piet, Felix, and I—set off in the dark to the dentist's office. As in the past, Piet walked ahead, with the two of us following him. It was a walk of at least forty-five minutes or more, and each minute seemed like hours. There were no back streets to take; each step was a grave risk. When we arrived, the dentist was waiting for us. The dentist appeared to be quite nervous and so, of course, were we.

"I better not turn on the lights; one never knows," the dentist said. "I can work by candlelight." Then turning to Piet and me, he said, "You two, please wait in the other room." He then lit some candles, and while Piet and I waited in another room, he worked on Felix. It took a long time, but finally Felix emerged minus one tooth, which the doctor had extracted. The doctor said, "Here are the medications that you must take as prescribed." We wanted to pay him for his services, but he refused. We shook hands again with him, and he wished the three of us good luck. He then said, "Remember, I have never seen you people, ever, in my life."

It had gotten quite late, and our next worry was walking the same distance home. The tension was unbearable; Felix with bloody cotton in his mouth; planes flying overhead; and Piet walking ahead of us. Finally we returned home safely, with Dina anxiously waiting for us with the customary surrogate tea. The medication that the dentist had given Felix worked, and in a few days he felt much better.

The air raids became more and more frequent. It was time to build an air raid shelter, Piet told us. Being an expert contractor, Piet knew exactly what to do and how to build one. Within a month he completed a shelter with water, food, and household items stored inside. He also made a contraption in the yard where we could hide Felix's diaries and my newspaper clippings, which were stored in metal boxes. He and Dina agreed that we should keep all documents because in the event that we should survive this ordeal, we could easily dig up the valuable papers. If not us, then someone would. We knew they had to be saved—they were history.

As spring began, we learned that my aunt and uncle had been deported; they were forced to leave their beloved Amersfoort on April 15, 1943. They had been born and raised there and happily lived with my grandparents. Their destination was—as we later learned—Sobibor and the gas chambers.

We had no idea what the fate was of those who had been deported. Though we understood that the Germans were malicious and had nothing good planned for those who ended up in concentration camps, we had no concept of what had really happened to these poor people. Our understanding began to heighten at the end of 1943. Jeroen stopped by one evening, and while he and Piet were talking in the hallway, I overheard him mention the words "gas chamber." We didn't understand the context of the conversation; however, we kept thinking about what Jeroen had meant. Because our minds could not perceive such evil, we dismissed the words from our thoughts.

Though I knew deep in my heart that neither my mother nor my other loved ones would be able to survive in a concentration camp for a long time, I still carried a flicker of hope that perhaps—against all odds—a miracle could happen and I would see my mother again.

Food became scarce. Somehow Piet and Dina knew how to buy what I called snakes, better known as eel. After the doors were locked and the curtains drawn, we helped them prepare the eel by cutting off their heads. The eel still wriggled around in the sink, even headless. I hated looking at them; it gave me the shivers. But Dina had a way of preparing them, and when dinner was served, I diverted my thoughts from the headless creatures and bravely ate my meal.

By the beginning of June 1943, the general health of the Dutch people had deteriorated. The Germans were sending large food supplies to Germany to feed their own people. It was around this time that the majority of the Dutch physicians sent a petition to Seyss-Inquart, still the head of the occupation troops in Holland. The petition was signed by hundreds of physicians. It was quite a courageous deed, considering the hateful mentality of the Nazis.

The petition appeared in the newspapers, and it was also distributed among people in the resistance. The document consisted of two pages, beautifully written in the Dutch language. Among other things, it stated that because of the scarcity of food, the spread of tuberculosis had become serious. Malnutrition among the Dutch was causing many deaths. The petition also mentioned the Treaty of 1907, executed in The Hague, clearly stating that no occupied country would suffer starvation on account of occupational troops.

Piet gave us a copy of this document, which Felix immediately put in our secret metal box; thus it was preserved for history. At the end of the letter the physicians appealed to the conscience of Seyss-Inquart.

The result was terrible. A great number of the physicians who signed the petition were deported to Germany, never to be heard from again.

One evening when the four of us were sitting together, Felix said, "You know, I just got an idea. Last year I saved for my cousins in Rotterdam—who are now safely in South America—all their valuable household effects, art and furniture. Mr. Loos is the man who helped me retrieve these things with his moving truck. Together, we brought all of these items to his home. He promised to hide everything in his attic, where it is safe. I remember what a dangerous mission that was. If I had left these goods in Rotterdam, I am sure the Germans would have found the house and emptied it by now. I'm convinced that Mr. Loos is a good patriotic citizen. He lives right near here. The time has come to get some extra food, and I'm willing to go to him and take some of the valuables out so that we can exchange it with the farmers for extra food. What do you think, Piet?"

Piet and Dina just nodded. Food was imperative to stay alive. The Van den Hoeven family now had five Jewish people in their home. They had taken in Kurt's mother, who had to move from her original hiding place in Baarn because of the elderly couple's illness.

All in all, there were now fourteen people who needed food. Though Piet was at first hesitant that Felix should go, the pros and cons were thoroughly discussed. If Piet should go, then Mr. Loos might become suspicious. But if Felix went, Mr. Loos would not get to know where Felix resided. And so the decision was that Felix would go. The next evening Felix left on Piet's bike. He went through the backyard, into the alley, and around the block to Mr. Loos's home. Before Felix left, Piet said to him, "I'll give you an hour. If you are not back by then, I will start looking for you. Be sure to have your papers with you."

I was afraid and couldn't help thinking, "What if ... what if ..." and attaching horrible things to the ends of those sentences, imagining Felix coming into all kinds of danger. Dina had made the sign of the cross when Felix left, as was her habit in dangerous situations. Somehow, that act had given me a kind of reassurance, which I could not explain.

In less than an hour Felix returned safe and sound, carrying a number of paintings and clothes. What a relief it was to see him! He told us that he had rung the bell at Mr. Loos's home, and when Mr. Loos answered the door he recognized Felix immediately. He guided Felix to the attic, never asking any questions.

The day before, Piet had made contact with some of the farmers living in Hoogland, a nearby village where they raised their crops. Our plan seemed to be working out well, and the next day Piet left early on his bike to Hoogland to exchange some items for food. Although the value of the paintings greatly exceeded not only the cost of the food but also the farmers' knowledge of their value, the food, to us, was more precious. And so Felix went to Mr. Loos's from time to time, after which Piet exchanged the items for food for the

Van den Hoevens and the Brandsens. We were grateful that all went well, while the food sustained all of us.

One day Piet came home with two large bags of beans. It was midsummer, and Piet suggested that the beans should be laid out on our balcony to dry. Dina helped to spread out the beans in their full glory. It was a sight to behold. There were enough beans to share with two families.

The next morning we suddenly heard a loud noise. I ran toward the balcony shouting, "Oh, the beans! It must be raining." Quickly opening the door, I saw there was no rain. It was Opa, who had thrown the contents of his chamber pot out of his window and onto the precious beans. We ran downstairs with great excitement, telling Dina and Piet what had happened. At first Piet made a joke of it, saying, "Oh, that Opa and his secret transmitters!" After they had come upstairs to see the mess, Piet said, "We can still eat them but not as they are now. We have to wash them off."

The next few hours were spent running up and down the stairs with buckets of water, trying to undo Opa's insolence. After all that, Piet motioned to Dina, saying, "Cook the beans a bit longer so that all of the germs are gone." Then he added, "You know what, cook them along with the eels. What's the difference, everything goes into one stomach anyway!"

I had always been extremely health conscious, but between the beans and the eels, and the tulip bulbs we occasionally had to eat, I rapidly lost weight. However, we were grateful for everything: for the kind Brandsen family, for the love and understanding they showed us, and for the Van den Hoeven family, who so graciously sheltered Felix's family. Before each meal I said a silent prayer of thanks in my own way.

+⸺⸺⸺+

The air raid shelter in the backyard was well used because much fighting went on in the skies above us while sirens blasted day and night. The Americans had begun their bombing by day over the occupied territories; unfortunately, at times they missed their targets and hit civilians. Many lives were lost. I was terrified every time I heard planes fly overhead. I would lose all composure, begin shaking and crying, and run in panic toward the air raid shelter. At times Felix became impatient with me. He said, "Let's be happy that the Americans are here; they are helping us to become free again."

One day, as the sirens began to blast again and the planes roared overhead, we all ran into the shelter. Suddenly the neighbors next door, the Kerkhof family, also came running in. We all huddled together, and after the all-clear signal had sounded, we left the shelter. As Mrs. Kerkhof took a look at Felix and me, Dina said, "These are two relatives from Belgium." With a good-natured gesture of her hand, Mrs. Kerkhof said, "Don't worry; everything is safe with us."

The Germans continued to issue new ordinances and laws that further terrorized the lives of all Dutch people. The Nazis instituted a Compulsory Work Program, requiring all citizens to work in Germany for the German war effort. Those who could not prove that they completed this work program were prevented from continuing their studies or their jobs. They also were not allowed to get food.

Men between the ages of twenty-two and forty were requisitioned to report to the German authorities, who would then transport them to Germany. Those men who were able to find hiding places disappeared. Piet reported that few men were seen on the streets anymore; Dina begged Piet to be careful during the day. He was thirty-eight years old—a prime age to be picked up by the Germans and deported. Ordinances always appeared with the typical German efficiency, along with the customary threats in case of noncompliance.

The Germans also ordered all Dutch to turn in their bank notes of one thousand and five hundred Dutch guilders. Piet and Felix explained to us that most probably the Germans wanted to prevent people from fleeing the country with large sums of money.

Worst of all were the announcements in the newspapers—sadistically summed-up reports of the executions of Dutch citizens. One of my February 2, 1943, newspaper clippings from The Hague reads as follows in German:

DER HÖHERE SS UND POLIZEIFÜHRER NORDWEST UND
GENERALKOMMISAR FÜR DAS SICHERHEITSWESEN GET.
RAUTER SS GRUPPENFÜHRER UND GENERAL-LEUTNANT
DER POLIZEI, MACHT BEKANNT ...

Translated, this means, "The highest SS and police commander of the Northwest [Holland] and the General for the Commissioner of the Security Department, Rauter, announce the following ..." Then followed the names, ages, and residences of people who were executed by the Germans. The Germans actually referred to them as "communist-inspired agitators."

The orders were always signed by Rauter (Hanns Albin Rauter), an Austrian SS officer who was assigned as Heinrich Himmler's principal representative in the Netherlands in 1940 for the purpose

of exterminating the Dutch Jews. Rauter committed the most heinous crimes in Holland for which he was promoted by Himmler to
the highest police rank as executor of the "final solution." Himmler,
of course, was one of Hitler's lieutenants and was called "The Butcher
of Europe's Jewry." Rauter regarded the extermination of the Jews as
a glorious chapter in Germany's history. After the war he was sen-
tenced to death by a Dutch court and executed in 1949. His boss,
Himmler, was captured by the British in 1945; he committed suicide that same year.

In that same year, 1943, the Germans ordered the closure of
theaters, restaurants, and any business they did not deem valuable
to their cause. In spite of the dismal circumstances, we all looked
forward to the evenings when we gathered to listen to the BBC. By
listening to the crystal radio, we learned that many German cities
such as Essen, München, and Berlin had been heavily bombed by
the Allies; the two cities of Wilhelmshaven and Cuxhaven were
totally destroyed. Despite all this, the Germans kept bragging in the
newspapers about their victories.

While the Germans had designed their Luftwaffe (air force)
to work closely with ground forces in their blitzkrieg (lightning
war), the Allies developed bombers that could fly long distances.
They could make daily raids over Europe.

In May of 1943 we found a most unusual piece of news in the
papers. The Germans had accused a Jewish person, a chemicals
specialist living in London, of being guilty of a terrorist attack on
the dams in Germany. Apparently, this air bombing had done so
much damage that the Nazis swore that in retaliation they would
punish all Jewish people who were still alive.

One evening in July, while we were sitting together, Dina served tea with cookies. I had not seen the cookies before, and, noticing my puzzled look, Dina said, "Tonight is special." She then looked at Piet, who walked to the sitting room, returning with a flower pot. He came over to Felix and me and with his customary humor sang "Happy Anniversary." He then handed me the flowers.

It was July 9, 1943, our wedding anniversary, which we both had apparently forgotten. Piet gave me a hug and shook hands with Felix; then, reaching into his pockets, he removed two letters and handed them to us. They were from Felix's family at the Van den Hoevens'. One was from Nel and Kurt and the other from Felix's mother, who wrote to us in beautiful German *Buchstaben,* a special style of written letters. They congratulated us on our one-year anniversary. We were very touched by the flowers, the cookies, and the letters, and we thanked the Brandsens for making the day so special for us under such difficult circumstances.

Piet reported that our family was fine. He had talked to Mr. and Mrs. Van den Hoeven, who told him that Felix's mother carried her prayer book with her everywhere and prayed constantly. Even when bombs were flying overhead and everyone huddled together downstairs, Felix's mother's trust in her faith was so strong that she stayed in her room and continued to pray.

In the meantime, Felix and I continued typing, sorting, and filing—in general, helping Piet in the resistance. One day, late in the afternoon, we had papers spread about the table in our bedroom. This could have been dangerous.

The Madonna was on the table amid all of the mess. On this day, as Felix and I worked away, Piet and Jeroen came up to our room. Suddenly Piet took the Madonna, saying, "You don't need this here; I'll take her downstairs so that you have more space."

To my surprise, I panicked and blurted out, "No, no—I want to keep her here." The three men looked absolutely puzzled, especially Felix.

Jeroen said good-naturedly, "Let her have it." Piet put the statue back on the table. I did not dare look at Felix.

Later that night I tried to think about it. My mind had become so twisted during those years. Most likely, I had connected the Madonna with my mother's image. Later in bed Felix and I talked about the incident. Felix said, "Everything is in the hands of God."

+>—+—<+

The hardships that everyone suffered during that long war became unbearable at times. The devious ordinances from the occupying forces affected every household, especially farmers. The Germans needed horses, cows, chickens, and other livestock, which they confiscated. In many instances they also took the farmhands, who were then transported to Germany to work. People who drove trucks for commercial purposes had to obtain applications to get permits for gasoline. They had to apply in person to the offices of German authorities and fill out endless forms. Many did not want to go; those who were fortunate enough to find hiding places disappeared.

Since 1942 the population had to deal with all kinds of substitutes for most edible items. For example, there were surrogates for tea, coffee, and tobacco. Every household was allotted only a small amount of food—truly minimal portions. For instance, one was allowed no more than two hundred fifty grams of bread and ten grams of flour. Sugar and butter or margarine were almost unobtainable. One-fourth of a liter of low-fat milk had to be sufficient for a family with children. One kilo of potatoes was a feast. Fish was free but only limited kinds.

Many families ran out of linens, blankets, and underwear. Shoes were no longer available, which was a tragedy for growing children. Felix learned how to patch up shoes with wooden soles for the four children. He became quite good at it, and it kept him busy. I had not seen stockings for three years and was always wearing my woolen knee-highs. Because of the lack of clothing, as well as the constant bombing, children could no longer go to school.

The beautiful carillons of the churches' bell towers were confiscated and sent to Germany to be made into weapons. The defenses that the Germans had built along the coast caused hundreds, if not thousands, of people to evacuate their homes.

Because of the nightly blackout, which had to be strictly observed, people often drowned in the many rivers and canals of the country. The farmers became besieged by the civilian population, who tried to exchange their meager possessions for food. People needed their bikes to go to the country, but the bikes now had wooden wheels, which made a terrible noise. Rubber tires did not exist any longer.

At times Dina and I felt like falling apart, but Piet and Felix kept up the good spirit, which was necessary for our daily struggle. Piet consoled me and said, "You have to grit your teeth and persevere. Holland shall be free!"

The bombings sometimes took place on Sundays, when the Allied forces knew people would not be working, for they wanted to avoid hitting civilians. Throughout this time, the Brandsen family bravely went to church. When the sirens began to blast, there was not much time to go to the attic and get Opa. We tried many times to get him downstairs, but he was not aware of what was going on and could barely hear.

Piet was fearless; he had nerves of steel. We were fascinated as we listened to his descriptions of the many heroic deeds the brave people of the resistance were performing throughout the country. I often became quite anxious about the consequences should any information leak out. I hung on to Felix for strength, especially when he uttered with confidence, "We have come so far now, we must go through with it. We must share our portion and do our part against the enemy."

And so the year 1943 dragged on. Christmas passed, and a new year dawned on us. When Piet sneaked to the Van den Hoevens' now and then, we exchanged letters with Felix's family. My mother-in-law, in her beautiful style of writing, had sent good wishes to us in September for Rosh Hashanah, for Hanukkah, and for the secular year 1944. We always guessed about the actual dates for the Jewish holidays, but we figured that September must be the Jewish New Year and Yom Kippur. Around Christmas it must be Hanukkah. As there was no formal printed calendar and we relied on our community rabbis for information, once deported, there was no official announcement of holidays for those of us left behind. Felix would remind me of these festivals, but to me during these years they did not mean anything.

During the last six months of 1943, Piet often came home late at night, having taken on important assignments that he would relate to us when he arrived. We were extremely busy with typing for the resistance. For these reasons we got into the habit of going back to our rooms at night after dinner to do some more work. We always waited until Piet came home, and after Dina's "the coast is clear" signal, we would go downstairs.

CHAPTER 11

A Night of Infamy

Piet Brandsen

January 21, 1944

One night we were working in our room upstairs when the red light went on. It was about six o'clock. A small heater was on, and spread out on the table was an array of illegal papers, food coupons, names and addresses, as well as a heap of *Parool* newspapers.

Suddenly we heard a terrific noise—yelling and screaming in German. It was the Gestapo, the dreaded German secret police. Felix, his face distorted in fear, motioned to me, then pointed toward the hiding cell. Gripped with panic and disbelief, we crawled into the place and—as the rehearsals had taught us—first locked the outside door and then the second inside door. There had been no time to hide any of the numerous papers on the table. The screaming downstairs was earsplitting. Even sequestered in our hiding cell, we could hear the intruders giving commands. We could only guess what was going on.

My nightmare had come true. We were face-to-face with the enemy. Our lives and that of the Brandsen family were over. My heart pounded uncontrollably, and I began to feel the claustrophobia take over. I clung to Felix, desperately gulping for more air, my mind going as a windmill in a storm. What would happen to Dina and the children? Where was Piet? How would the confrontation go when the Gestapo found us? I was desperate to unlock the doors and get out of there. Felix had to hold me back; I felt as if I had gone out of my mind.

Suddenly we heard footsteps coming up the staircase. We knew exactly how many steps there were. As the person arrived at the top stair and reached for the doorknob, a voice from below yelled out in German, "Was suchen Sie da, es gibt ja nichts da oben." Translated, this means, "What are you doing there, there is nothing upstairs." It must have been the head officer of the group, who wanted to show his superiority toward his subordinate; such was a characteristic of the "master race." We heard him go down the steps again, whereupon the yelling resumed. Clearly, the secret police were waiting for Piet.

As the fearful noise continued, we heard furniture being thrown, people stomping through rooms, Dina being ordered about. The minutes leaped into hours. What if the SS found the crystal radio or the secret papers? Where was Piet, and how were Dina and the children holding up?

Holding on to each other, Felix and I kissed each other good-bye, just as my sister had kissed me the day the German troops marched in; it seemed so long ago now. Felix began whispering the Kaddish, the prayer of mourning for the dead. In this prayer there are no complaints, only praise for God and for his wisdom. He also recited the Shema, the prayer of affirmation of our faith. My mind bounced back and forth from one terrifying thought to another as I gasped for air. My thinking was so distorted that in one moment I hoped that I would meet my mother in heaven, and in the next I pictured Piet in danger or dreamed how it would be to find freedom again.

Finally, finally, there was silence. We heard someone in our room, then the voice of Dina calling out to us. After we crawled out of our cell, we looked at her face. Instantly we knew that a tragedy had occurred. Her face looked ashen, and tears were streaming down her cheeks. In between her sobs she said, "They have taken Piet; he had *Het Parool* in his pocket. They also arrested Piet Kerkhof, the neighbor's son, who came in to listen to the crystal radio. The Gestapo asked him what he was doing here, and he said he came over to borrow a book. They also took him to a concentration camp."

With a gesture of despair, she continued, "There were two SS officers, and one NSB. The NSB officer was the one who had climbed the stairs to your room but was ordered to come back down."

Both Dina and I cried in desperation. Felix quickly picked up all the papers from the table and put them in the hiding place. The three of us stood there in a tight embrace, trying to absorb the tragedy that had taken place. Felix's face was stricken with sorrow. He said, "We cannot stay here any longer. They might come back to search the entire house."

Dina nodded, saying, "You cannot leave through the front door or the back door." She was right. The Germans had a habit of coming right back after a razzia or committing another crime. It was their way of slyly investigating other things that may have been going on against their ordinances.

Felix and I asked in a worried tone, "Where are the children? Are they all right?"

Dina nodded. "I sent them to the neighbors'."

There was no more time to waste; we could stay no longer because our secret presence was a danger. Hugging us tightly, Dina uttered these last words to us: "I know a man who sometimes brought food to us. He knew that you were hidden here; they are good people and live in the outskirts somewhere, but it is far from here. His name is Hornsveld."

Our dear Piet had been betrayed for his work in the resistance movement. We wanted to ask Dina a thousand questions, but she had already left the room. We had to hurry—there was no time for questions anymore.

In a daze, we quickly put on our coats and went to the balcony off our room. Outside it was icy cold and pitch-dark. We stood on the balcony for a few minutes, not knowing what to do or where to go.

We knew that there was a gutter pipe on the left side of the balcony. Felix whispered to me to follow him as he climbed over the balcony railing and began to slide down the gutter. As if in a dream I followed him, and although I could hardly see a thing I too went over the railing and slid down the gutter pipe.

Within a few minutes we stood on the ground. Taking a huge risk, we sneaked into the backyard and then into the alley. Shivering from the bitter cold, Felix whispered, "We must reach the Van den Hoevens." We had met Mr. Van den Hoeven on a few occasions in the Brandsens' home, but we did not know where his house was. All we knew was that he lived on the same street as Piet and Dina.

One way or the other, we had to go back to the street. Searchlights streamed from the sky as the Germans scoured the air for Allied planes. For a moment, in my utter confusion, I hoped for the bombings—perhaps, I thought, it would end this horrible nightmare I was living. Finally we reached the street, struggling through the slippery ground. A number of Dutch homes had entry doorways at that time. Each time a searchlight lit up the street, we hid in the doorway of a house, just like thieves. Felix whispered to me, "We can't go on like this. We have to ring a doorbell somewhere." We held on to each other, saying a silent prayer.

Taking a terrific chance, we rang the doorbell of the next house. A male voice called out, "Who is there?"

Felix replied, with a quivering voice, "Piet Brandsen has been taken away by the Gestapo."

Slowly the door opened, and yet another miracle occurred. It was Mr. Van den Hoeven. Our prayers had been heard. By the grace of God we had rung the right doorbell. Mr. Van den Hoeven said, "Come in quickly, before someone sees!"

With an alarmed expression on his face, Mr. Van den Hoeven asked us what had happened. After we told him he just kept repeating,

"Oh, my God, oh, my God." In the meantime, Mrs. Van den Hoeven had come to the hallway where we were standing. When she heard about the tragedy, she too became terrified; with her hands over her face, she kept lamenting and crying. Then an uncomfortable silence took over. Felix and I, in this desperate situation, could not say a word. We realized that our lives depended on what would take place within the next few minutes.

Finally Mr. Van den Hoeven said, "We cannot have any more people in the house; as it is now, we already have five people here hiding." I was shaking uncontrollably, both from the cold and from my emotions. I said, "Dina mentioned the name of Hornsveld; he sometimes brought food, but we don't know where he lives."

Turning to his wife, Mr. Van den Hoeven nodded. "Yes, of course, I know where he lives. I was in his home a few times with Piet." First he looked at his wife, then at us. Then, as if he had suddenly come to a decision, he said to us, "You know what? I will take you to the Hornsvelds'. There is no other way." I saw Mrs. Van den Hoeven's face turn from white to ashen. Although she did not object to her husband's proposal, she did say, "Please be careful; you know there is a curfew on."

It is difficult to describe our state of mind that night. We felt guilty for bringing others into danger; we feared for our lives. We felt as if we were a burden to people who, in essence, were total strangers. The anxiety was overwhelming.

As Mr. Van den Hoeven took a coat out of the hall closet, Mrs. Van den Hoeven motioned to us, saying, "Come upstairs with me; you have to say hello to your family. But please, make it short." We followed her up the steps, and as she opened a door, we saw our family members: Kurt, Nel, Felix's mother, and Kurt's mother. They were all lying on the bed. Needless to say, they were shocked to see us and to hear about the most recent tragedy. We quickly said hello and, just as quickly, good-bye. Felix's mother, who was holding a prayer book, put it down. She then placed her hands on our heads and recited a blessing in Hebrew. She cried softly.

Back in the downstairs hallway, Mr. Van den Hoeven said, "Well, let's go. I will walk ahead of you; the two of you must follow me. Be prepared that this is a dangerous undertaking." Before he opened the door, he took our hands and said, "Let's bow our heads and ask the Almighty for his blessing."

Mr. Van den Hoeven, an elderly man, had a difficult time walking against the raw, chilly wind. He could not be seen with a Jewish couple, so he walked a bit ahead of us. Now and then, when the coast was clear, he waited for us, offering encouraging words. We passed by a number of canals, which we could faintly detect in the dark. After we had passed an ancient castle, we came to what looked like empty terrain. Mr. Van den Hoeven seemed to know his way around; we continued to follow him through a narrow inlet. Finally, we approached a large house.

Mr. Van den Hoeven rang the bell. We heard footsteps, then the voice of a woman. "Who is it?" she asked.

"It is Van den Hoeven. I am here with a young couple. Piet Brandsen was arrested by the German police." The door opened slightly. Mr. Van den Hoeven stepped in, saying, "I have here a young Jewish couple. They need to stay overnight somewhere."

We stepped into the house, then the woman carefully locked the door. "This is Jan and Marietje," Mr. Van den Hoeven said. "They have nowhere to go. Please, could you have them over for one night?" Poor Mr. Van den Hoeven had a difficult time catching his breath as he explained.

Mrs. Hornsveld, a serious-looking, heavyset woman of about forty, put her hand to her face and lamented, "Oh, how terrible! Poor Brandsen, and what about his wife and the four children?"

A shattering silence took over. She finally said, "My husband and my oldest son are not here right now, but I will talk to my youngest son." She went to one of the rooms in the back of the hall, and we heard her say, "Bertus, come here. Piet Brandsen was arrested by the Germans."

A young man in his teens appeared. Mr. Van den Hoeven began to explain again what had happened. As I listened again, I wished for the ground to open up and swallow me right then and there. Then I heard Mrs. Hornsveld ask her son, "Can we have them for one night?" Bertus quickly answered, "Yes, we can!" We did not know it then, but his answer had determined our future forever.

After Mr. Van den Hoeven left Mrs. Hornsveld brought us into her front room and told us that her family knew all along that we were hiding at the Brandsen home. On several occasions Mr. Hornsveld had brought extra food to the Brandsen family, which Piet had shared with the Van den Hoevens. She explained that they too were helping with the underground movement by taking care of patriotic citizens whose husbands or sons had fallen prey to the Nazis. Both of her sons were involved.

Finally, she guided us upstairs to a room that had a window facing the back of the property. She said, "Listen carefully because what I am going to say is very important." She motioned toward the window and continued, "Here is the river, the Eem. Across from the river is the headquarters of the Gestapo. You must keep the curtains drawn. You must stay upstairs at all times because we have an office in our home downstairs with employees who must not know that you are here. My husband will explain everything to you tomorrow."

After that, she handed us some bed linens and blankets and wished us good night. I said to Felix, "What now?"

He said again to me, "We are just in the hands of God."

I kept thinking, "I have abandoned God these past two years, and here we are, our prayers for help answered." Contemplating our uncertain future, I mentioned to Felix the subject of God. Fate meant for us to stay alive—so far. But at the same time, I felt that my mother was gone forever. My thoughts went out again to all those who had been deported. What had become of them? Was God watching over them? What about our courageous Piet, held in a concentration camp? We prayed intensely that night that his life would be spared.

Then Felix said with a determined tone in his voice, "It is now Friday night, January 21, 1944. The Shabbat has begun. I am going to make a vow: I pledge to God that if we survive, I will do anything to keep the Jewish people together, wherever they might be in the world." His voice was trembling, and the emotion of that moment touched my heart deeply.

I asked God for forgiveness for my indifference over the past years. Holding hands, Felix and I prayed for courage to face the future. I remembered the words of the Hornsvelds' young son. In later years, "Yes, we can," would become the opening phrase of my lectures about the Holocaust.

+≡⇒+

Very early in the morning we heard a knock on the door. It was Mrs. Hornsveld, who greeted us amicably and said, "You better come downstairs and have something to eat before the office help comes in." We followed her down the stairs to the large living room, where we had been the night before.

A lovely little girl was seated at the table. Mrs. Hornsveld said to us, "This is Corrie, our twelve-year-old daughter. She loves to sketch as you can see from her drawings here on the table." Turning to Corrie she said, "This is Jan and Marietje. They stayed here overnight because Mr. Brandsen is in a concentration camp and they could not stay at the Brandsen home any longer."

Corrie simply smiled at us; we could see that she did not fully understand the situation. She was endowed with beautiful blond hair, a gorgeous complexion, and a captivating smile. A few minutes after our introduction to Corrie, her brother Bertus came into the room, greeting us with a cheery "good morning."

Corrie, in her childish innocence, wanted to show us around the outside of the home, but Mrs. Hornsveld explained emphatically that from now on everyone in the house was to be very careful and discreet. She then took us to the office, which had a large window, to show us what the surroundings were like.

The house was very big and situated next to a large lumber-yard, which Mr. Hornsveld managed. Behind the lumberyard was a body of water in which a number of small boats sat. Beyond was a meadow where cows and horses grazed. The environment looked charming. It was, by all standards, a typical, peaceful Dutch land-scape, worthy of a painting by one of Holland's great artists. It was snowing lightly outside which added more charm to the scene.

We were on the outskirts of town, and we realized, after seeing our surroundings, what a long walk it had been that terrible night from the Van den Hoevens' to the Hornsvelds'. We hoped that Mr. Van den Hoeven made it back safely to his home.

Bertus explained to us that a big building to the right of the lumberyard had been a crate factory, which the Germans had closed down. It was now used as a storage facility for hiding per-sonal automobiles. Beyond were some neighbors and, farther down, a tiny convenience store owned by a family named Bakker. The owner delivered his wares on a tricycle.

With the Gestapo headquarters across the river and the office personnel being unreliable, we were fully aware of the dangers of our hiding at the Hornsvelds'.

By now it was time for us to go upstairs to our room and wait with much anxiety for Mr. Hornsveld. We felt extremely fearful for ourselves as well as for this family, who had suddenly found themselves with two strangers—not only a strange couple, but a Jewish couple, at a time when Jews were not supposed to be in ex-istence in Holland any longer. We wondered how Mr. Hornsveld would react to us when he came home.

We had heard from Piet that some people, on impulse and from the kindness of their hearts, had taken in persecuted people, not thinking of the reality of the danger. In some cases it did not work out and the situations had ended in great tragedy. All these thoughts weighed heavily on our minds. Suddenly a knock came at the door. A jolly-looking, rather portly man in his forties introduced himself as Henk Hornsveld. We shook hands, and as he seated himself on the bed we began to talk. He said that he had known all along that we were hiding at the Brandsen home and that he was also working for "the cause" as a patriotic Dutch citizen. He expressed shock and regret over Piet's arrest by the Germans. We all talked of our worry about his fate and that of Dina and the children. For a while the three of us were silent, in deep thought over our conversation.

Felix broke the silence by saying, "Mr. Hornsveld, we cannot begin to tell you how very concerned and sorry we are to put you and your family in such a dilemma, but we have nowhere to go." Mr. Hornsveld nodded sympathetically, although we detected some uncertainty in his facial expression; we fully understood his concern. For a few moments not a word was spoken—what could any of us say?

But then, as Mr. Hornsveld was getting up from the bed, he said, "Let's try it out and see how it will work." This was the last we heard about this dilemma, from either Mr. or Mrs. Hornsveld. As he was about to leave, he spoke these words, which I have never forgotten: "I don't expect less from myself than doing my utmost for my fellow man as a patriotic citizen."

Later that evening as we sat down to dinner with the family, the conversation again turned to the Brandsen family and to Piet in particular. Mr. Hornsveld said, "I will go to Dina and see if she needs help. You probably need your clothes and other things. I will pick them up for you."

I suddenly blurted out, "Oh, Mr. Hornsveld, all of our important documents and paper clippings are there! Our wedding papers and my mother's farewell letter and ..." I began to stutter. "Everything in the metal boxes in Piet's backyard ..." Now I began to cry bitterly. "Please ask Dina to save them." Mr. Hornsveld put his arms around me, assuring me that he would do his best. He said, "Just be calm." As an afterthought he added, "I am sure that Holland will be free again someday." Upon hearing the word *free*, I got hold of myself and peace seemed to return to the dinner table.

The next morning something worrisome happened again. After breakfast, as Felix and I tiptoed through the hallway to go to our room upstairs, we ran into a person we had not seen before. It happened to be a salesman who worked for Mr. Hornsveld; he identified himself as Van Nus. We could tell by the look on his face that he figured out what was going on—the Hornsvelds were hiding a Jewish couple.

Mr. and Mrs. Hornsveld, who were in the hallway with us, looked quite concerned. Mr. Hornsveld began to explain in a calm tone that we were their guests from up north, but Van Nus, who was obviously a smart fellow, looked carefully at us and then at Mr. and Mrs. Hornsveld. As Mr. Hornsveld was telling a story, Van Nus interrupted him, winked, and said, "Ja, ja, ja."

As Felix and I were standing forlornly in that hallway, Mrs. Hornsveld turned to Van Nus and with a no-nonsense tone said, "Look, this couple is here with us for now, and I expect total discretion from you."

Van Nus nodded, but he managed to ask, "What are their plans? Where are they going from here?"

Again, we were in the hands of a higher power. It was the worst question anyone could ask us during our odyssey through the Holocaust. Van Nus disappeared into the office, and we never saw him again. The incident was never again mentioned.

٭══٭

A few days later we met Hannie, the oldest son. He was a sturdy, buoyant-looking young man with a healthy, outdoors complexion. The office personnel had left, and we all sat down in the living room. Mr. and Mrs. Hornsveld began to explain what had happened and how Felix and I came to be there. Hannie nodded his head with an understanding expression on his face.

There was a lot to discuss, and the parents wanted to point out to Hannie all of the dangers and problems associated with hiding us. There was a long list of things to consider: extra food coupons, the office staff, people coming in and out of the house, access to the air raid shelter. In short, things that were crucial to survival at that time could be thwarted by our presence.

After hearing about the risks, Hannie finally got up and said, "They must stay here; they are very welcome. I want only pros, no cons."

Then everyone in the room shouted, "Pros only, no cons!" The experience of that afternoon is engraved in our hearts; it gave us a tremendous boost to know that the whole family was of one mind and spirit in hiding us from the horrid Nazis.

That evening Bertus asked his family, "What about Gerrie and Hisje?" Gerrie and Hisje were his and his brother's girlfriends; they lived on a farm in a neighboring village and occasionally came to the Hornsveld home to visit and bring food. We learned that because the girls came a great distance on their bikes, they often stayed the night. Mrs. Hornsveld, looking at her sons, said, "Let's wait until they come and then decide what to do and how to do it."

Then Mr. Hornsveld asked to speak with us privately. He told us he had visited Dina Brandsen, and he assured us that she was doing the best she could under the circumstances. He told us that all of our paper clippings and documents were safe in the metal boxes hidden in the ground. We learned that the Van den Hoevens and Felix's family were doing all right. Mr. Hornsveld had also brought us some clothes, for which we thanked him profusely.

One advantage of the Hornsveld home was a second, small staircase leading from our room directly into the kitchen. Consequently, we did not have to be cooped up all day although we had to constantly be on the alert for strangers and the office staff. We had to be careful all of the time, as we had to use the same bathroom as the office staff. When the coast was clear, we would descend the stairs, sneak into the kitchen, and help Mrs. Hornsveld.

The Hornsvelds also had a crystal radio in the attic. At nightfall we would go upstairs and listen to the BBC with the boys. It was the *Voice of the Free World*, and we always hoped and prayed for good news.

Since the house was located near a railroad station, much fighting went on during the daytime with sirens blasting constantly as fighter planes flew over us. The large air raid shelter was located in the field to the left of the house, and each time the alarm went off, the neighbors came running. Of course, we stayed indoors because no one was to know we were there. We would go to the cellar for protection, but my claustrophobia was so overwhelming that most of the time during the air raids I ran to the front entrance of the home and stood in panic near the door.

The Hornsveld family was wonderful to us; in just a short time they made us feel like family members. However, we had not yet met the sons' girlfriends. Felix and I had been with the Hornsvelds for two weeks, but the girlfriends had not ventured out to visit because it was so dangerous to ride ramshackle bicycles when bombings were going on during the day. Mr. Hornsveld, knowing the girls would finally visit within a short time, said to the boys, "We must tell the girls about Jan and Marietje; they have to know the truth. There are no two ways about it."

Finally one afternoon Gerrie, Bertus's girlfriend, came to visit. Corrie called Felix and me to come down from our room to meet her. Gerrie was eighteen years old and very friendly looking. Her face glowed from the cold air and the long bike ride. When she first met us she looked surprised but did not ask any questions about us. She finally said, "Hisje will be here too." Mr. Hornsveld said, "Let's wait for Hisje; then we can explain everything."

We were all sitting in the living room when the doorbell rang. It was Hisje, a pretty girl of seventeen. She joined us in the living room.

Mr. Hornsveld then told the girls who we were, the events that had taken place, and the circumstances that led to our hiding in their home. Gerrie, Bertus's girlfriend, took it all quite calmly. But Hisje became so nervous that she pulled most of the buttons off her dress as she listened to the story.

Mrs. Hornsveld, a great diplomat and a gracious hostess, began to serve tea. With a fire roaring in the fireplace, the curtains drawn, and lights shining softly in the room, we all talked. Soon Hisje calmed down.

At last Mr. Hornsveld looked at Gerrie and Hisje and admonished, "Do not mention a word to your families. All of our lives depend on your secrecy." After the two young girls gave their promise not to utter a word to anyone, they came over and gave Felix and me a hug. They exuded honesty and kindness. We liked them immediately and found them to be trustworthy young women.

Mr. Hornsveld continued talking, looking now at his sons. He said, "We need hiding places." The boys nodded. Hannie said, "We can use the space underneath the small staircase. We should start right away and take some measurements." Mr. Hornsveld and his sons luckily had built boats and knew all about construction.

Suddenly we heard planes overhead, and the alarms began to sound. The ominous noise of the sirens along with the tumultuous roar of the approaching planes caused the family to run to the air raid shelter. The noise was earsplitting. Felix pulled me by the arm, and we ran to the cellar. The bombing and fighting going on over our heads seemed endless. I could not stand it any longer, and I ran out of the cellar into the hallway and toward the front entrance near the door. Suddenly there was a loud and heavy thud—similar to the sound of a thunderbolt. Felix came running down the hall. He wanted me to come back into the cellar, but I was so frightened I was afraid I would suffocate down there. After what seemed like hours, the all-clear signal sounded and the family emerged from the shelter.

Large pieces of metal from an airplane had plunged right in front of the door behind which I was standing, just a few feet away. If these pieces had landed any closer I would have been dead. We stood there with the family, looking at the large pieces of metal for a long time; all of us were in shock. The men were trying to figure out whether the pieces were from an Allied plane or a German plane that had crashed; they were anxious to know where it had come down.

Mrs. Hornsveld finally came forward and with a stern expression on her face said, "This is it. From now on I want Jan and Marietje in the shelter also. If something bad happens we don't want that on our conscience."

Everyone agreed. Mr. Hornsveld added, "Absolutely, Ma is right. We'll think of something to explain to the neighbors. I'll work something out."

<hr />

In a relatively short time Mr. Hornsveld and his sons had constructed several hiding places. Since the house was very large and old, it was easy to find spaces for hiding; the many nooks and crannies offered suitable places for this purpose.

We now had one hiding place upstairs that was easy to approach from our room in case something suspicious went on downstairs. Underneath the small staircase near the kitchen was a large, secret space. One had to crawl in this space and place a wood barrier over the opening. There was also a huge space in the attic. Two people could easily hide and sleep in there. In the event of danger, a hatch was closed from the inside, a rug was thrown over it, and no one would suspect that people could be in there.

Mr. and Mrs. Hornsveld suggested that we call them aunt and uncle, and so they became "Tante Cor and Oom Henk" (Aunt Cor and Uncle Henk). It came easily to us because we had become quite attached to the family. We did not know how to express our gratitude for all they did for us; we tried to make ourselves as useful as possible. I especially tried to be useful in the kitchen; after all, I was the "niece."

We learned from the BBC that the war was escalating. Hundreds, perhaps thousands, of Allied planes buzzed over our roof every night, always at the same time. We heard about the terrific bombing of strategic points in Germany. I was both fearful and happy to hear them fly over our heads: fearful that they would be shot down, happy to know they were bombing the barbaric enemy.

In late February 1944 the Allied air forces blasted industrial targets in Germany, such as railroads and factories. We heard through the crystal radio that these bombings would change the history of the war. Aircraft plants and many important factories in the major cities in Germany were destroyed. The Germans became frantic for workers to such an extent that they began to pick up anybody from the streets. On orders from Seyss-Inquart, people had to be deported to work for the war machine. No one was safe any longer. The Germans used the same tactics on non-Jews that they had used on the Jewish population.

We knew that Uncle Henk was deeply involved with the resistance, but contrary to Piet's openness, Oom Henk was very secretive about it. The only thing he had mentioned to us was that the newspaper, *Het Parool*, had continued to be printed and circulated in Amersfoort. No suspicion about this could fall on Piet. But none of us even knew where Piet was or how he was faring.

One evening at dinner Uncle Henk said in a quiet tone, "Before another huge bombardment comes along and we have to go into the shelter with the neighbors, I must tell you that I confided to some friends that you two are hiding in our home." I turned pale as he continued, "Marietje, calm yourself. I have some positive news to go along with this." We held our breath as we waited for his next words. He said, "I have a uniform for Jan. It is a clever idea because the uniform can function as a postman's as well as a German soldier's. Let me show you what it looks like."

Uncle Henk then left the room and shortly returned with a package. Out came a uniform. He said, "Come on, Jan, let's go upstairs and see if it fits you." Felix and I were stunned into silence, but Felix followed Uncle Henk.

After a short while the door opened, and there was Felix in a German officer's uniform. He could truly have posed for a German. Uncle Henk remarked, "You know, whoever made this was very, very smart because it fits Jan to a tee." He then reached into the package, and out came a number of interchangeable accessories. Inside the air raid shelter, Felix could be a postman.

The weather was still bitter cold, a thin layer of ice remaining on the river. With the approval of Uncle Henk and Aunt Cor, we'd open the front door at night to get some fresh air; we had been confined to the indoors for so long that we needed to get away from our upstairs room now and then. We frequently did exercises and deep breathing during these nights, with young Corrie on the lookout for strangers.

One evening as we were standing outside, we suddenly heard a man screaming loudly for help in German. A drunk German officer had fallen into the river. When we saw the neighbors come running down toward the river because of the commotion, Felix and I dashed upstairs. Koen, a neighbor who was the skipper for the freight boat, and Hannie had been working on the boat, which was moored to the back of the house. We lifted the curtains just a little to see what was happening.

We then saw Hannie—who was always eager to help—jump into the water to try to save the man. All the while we heard neighbors shouting obscenities, yelling for Hannie to throw the German back into the canal. While Koen and Hannie hoisted the German onto the boat, the soldier kept jabbering about his cap, which was in the water. We later learned that in the German army it is a big offense to lose one's cap.

Against all logic, Hannie brought the man into the house to a room downstairs. The man, shivering badly, stammered, "Heiss, heiss," meaning "hot, hot." Hannie quickly gave him some dry clothes and ordered a cab for him. The man was a sergeant stationed at the Dumoulin barracks in Soesterberg. The next day the German came back to the house with a coupon for Hannie to purchase shoes as replacement for the shoes that had ended up in the river.

It is not difficult to imagine the impression this event had on all of us. Should Hannie have let him drown? Had he done the right thing to save the enemy? Had he compromised, or was saving the

German the only option? This was the topic of discussion many times. Hannie had saved one life, but the enemy had taken millions.

After many discussions Uncle Henk said, "Look, if a similar situation happens again, we must simply stay out of it. Many people drown in the canals at night when it is dark. We must not continue to dwell on this." Turning to Hannie, Henk said, "I want to remind you that we have two people hiding here, so think about that in the future."

Several weeks later another German, an SS officer from the secret police, fell into the river and drowned. There was no one near to save him. In revenge, the Gestapo lined up seven innocent civilians and executed them on the spot in view of people who were ordered to watch. Such was the barbaric act of the German "master race."

Shortly after this incident we had to go into the shelter. The bombings were now continuous. We could see planes burning in the air, plunging to the ground not far from the house. The first time Felix entered the shelter in his uniform, someone asked, "Where are you from, and who are you?" Before he could answer, the tumult of the bombings drowned out all other sound; it was terrifying. Some of the neighbors were praying; all of us were panic-stricken, hoping to survive. When the bombings stopped, not one of the neighbors asked Felix any further questions. All of us were aware that the Allies were helping us and that eventually the liberation would come.

CHAPTER 12

Miracles Do Happen

*The back of the Hornsveld home and the open window of the room
where we were hiding, which faced Gestapo headquarters*

Since we could not work for *Het Parool* any longer, the days
upstairs became excruciatingly long. Felix still kept his diary,
but that did not take up much time. We hid the notes to the diary
in the hiding place near our room.

One day Felix asked Uncle Henk if there was anything he could
do that would occupy his time. Perhaps there was something special
he could think of. Uncle Henk understood fully how slowly the
days were going by for Felix, and he said, "Let me think about it;
maybe I might know of something." I kept myself useful by helping
Aunt Cor in the kitchen or doing sewing work or other household
chores. For me, the days went by much faster.

A few days later Uncle Henk came to us with a triumphant look on his face. He said, "Jan, by golly I have found something for you to do. Come to the attic and I'll show you what it is." When we got to the attic, we saw lots of colorful tiles and a heap of cement on the floor. Uncle Henk said, "I will show you and explain what can be done with all of that. The days will fly by for you!" He then showed Felix how to work the cement and the tiles so that one could make colorful flowerpots out of them.

From then on Felix spent days on end in the attic. In time, he became an expert at making flower pots, ashtrays, and many items that were useful for a household. In fact, he became so experienced and innovative with this hobby that Uncle Henk saw fit to sell the items or exchange them for food. At times even the air raids could not deter Felix from leaving the attic.

Despite the fact that this work gave both of us some peace of mind, everyone in the household had to be constantly on guard, and each of us was always edgy, not knowing what the Germans had in mind.

But luckily, one day we heard on the crystal radio that the Russians, who had recaptured Kiev at the end of 1943, had now broken the siege of Leningrad. When Felix predicted with certainty that Germany would lose the war, I began to feel somewhat less lethargic, and I began to daydream of freedom and how it would feel for life to be normal again.

Then, on Tuesday, June 6, 1944, we heard the exciting news that made us realize that the course of the war—and our lives— would change. It was a day never to be forgotten.

The men had gone upstairs to listen to the crystal radio while Aunt Cor and I were downstairs repairing some clothes. Corrie was drawing and making sketches. Suddenly Felix came running downstairs and into the room we were in with full speed, his eyes open wide with excitement, his face glowing. "Come quick, hurry up!" Felix shouted. "The Allies have landed in Normandy!"

We threw our sewing to the floor and in a frenzy ran upstairs. And there we heard it: the announcer from England broke the news, "The Allies have landed in Normandy!"

These words were repeated over and over again. Even though there was a lot of static and creaking on the little radio, we continued to listen and savor the words, not wanting to lose one syllable from this incredible news. Everything, it seemed, took on a new meaning, imbuing us with renewed hope.

However, just as we were basking in the hope for freedom, something again happened. About a week after the good news of the Allies landing in Normandy, while we were sitting at dinner we heard an ominous roar outside. We had never heard such an eerie sound before. All of us flew out of the room in different directions. I landed in the WC, which had a small window through which I could look outside. We saw a huge object with a great flame on its tail roaring over our area; the sound was unearthly. Then the sound stopped suddenly and we heard an enormous explosion nearby. It instantly reminded me of the explosion on the SS *Simon Bolivar*. There had been no air raid warning. Just the same, everyone ran into the air raid shelter, even Felix without his uniform.

We did not know what the thing was and where it had come from; for certain, it was not an airplane. Just as we were about to leave the shelter, a second object roared by with tremendous speed. That too exploded near our area.

The neighbors started to talk with each other, and one of them began to curse. "Damn," he shouted, "when will the war ever end!"

Then another person came forward and said, "It must be a rocket.... We must find out where it exploded."

But the next day we learned that the Germans had fired missiles; they were called V-1s. This news was all over the papers; the Germans were quite proud of their attacks. Now the horror of the missiles continued on a daily basis. We soon learned that when the sound stopped, the missile would soon explode. It would then hit civilians, who suffered great loss of life.

For the time being, our joyous expectations for freedom were gone. Every day I spent hours of agony in the bathroom, listening and waiting for missiles. Later on the Germans developed even stronger missiles, called V-2s. They were much bigger, like flying monsters that roared with huge flames through the air.

Uncle Henk learned that the missiles were fired not far off from where we lived and that V-2s could travel faster than the speed of sound. It was fearsome because we could not hear them coming— they zoomed by in a second. Through the BBC, we learned that the missiles could reach a height of sixty miles and then suddenly dive toward their target.

At night I stayed awake listening for those dreaded missiles. Added to this was the sound of the Allied planes flying over our heads by the hundreds. It was a living nightmare. One night in desperation I said to Felix, "I can't stand it any longer. Bring me poison!"

Felix became upset, saying, "Don't give up now; get a hold of yourself. The end of the war is near, and you have to grit your teeth." I tried hard not to show my fear to the Hornsvelds; yet again I lost weight because I could not eat or sleep.

We learned from the BBC that the missiles had reached London for the first time in June 1944, causing tremendous damage. We all felt great compassion for the brave people of England, and we greatly admired their perseverance despite the unimaginable air attacks they suffered.

Meanwhile we held fast to the news. We learned that the United States forces had broken out of Normandy and that Romania and Bulgaria had declared war on Germany. That little radio was truly our salvation, and it gave me a reason to pull myself together.

I spent the nights alone in our room because the family wanted Felix and the boys hidden; they feared the boys would be forced to serve in the German army if found. Felix and Bertus slept together in the large space in the ceiling. Hannie, who was home now, slept in the hiding place underneath the stairway on the first floor.

We could tell from the actions of the Germans and also from the information in the newspapers that the enemy had become reckless. They were indifferent to the suffering of the population and indiscriminate in shooting off their rockets. Food became very scarce, almost unobtainable.

All of us reached a low point, not knowing how long this infernal war would last. But on July 18, 1944, some very good news reached us. We heard on the BBC that the U.S. Army, led by General Omar Bradley, had broken out of Normandy's peninsula and was sweeping across France. Then on the evening of July 20, 1944, the most unbelievable news of all was reported on the radio. A German by the name of Colonel Count von Stauffenberg had tried to assassinate Hitler, placing a time bomb under Hitler's table during a staff meeting. Unfortunately, Hitler had only been slightly wounded. We hoped that this would be the end of the war, but Von Stauffenberg, after being brutally tortured by his own people, was executed.

Immediately following all of these highly emotional events, Felix became quite ill. He developed a high fever; his lips, eyes, and entire face swelled up so badly that he looked grotesque. All of the pressures, tensions, and anxieties seemed to have come to a head. It was clear that a doctor had to be called.

A doctor came to the house to check on Felix that evening. The family had assured us that Dr. Plomp was a good, patriotic person. He seemed friendly and relaxed as he shook hands with us. I was present as the Hornsvelds explained to the doctor who we were and how we got there.

I followed the doctor upstairs. After he examined Felix thoroughly, he turned to me and said, "Your husband has urticaria; it is an allergic reaction." He indicated to Felix that he would be back in a few days and then said to me, "I will talk to you downstairs." Upon reaching the large hallway, Dr. Plomp said to me, "Your husband is very sick. He needs complete rest and special food. He is young and will make it, but he needs care. As much as possible, keep him away from worrisome news."

The doctor also spoke with the Hornsvelds. It gave me a good feeling to know that he would be back again to check on Felix. As he was leaving, he said to me in Dutch (loosely translated), "Hold on tight, freedom is around the corner!"

To become so ill while in hiding and to be so dependent upon strangers was very difficult, to say the least. But somehow we had been blessed with encountering such good people along the way, people who had shown compassion and love for their fellow citizens.

When I came downstairs the next morning for breakfast, I asked, "Where is Uncle Henk?" The family told me that he had left very early that morning for nearby farms to secure special food for Felix. I was truly moved, almost to tears.

Up until now, there had been adequate food for all of us at the Hornsveld home. However, eggs, milk, and meat were almost unattainable. A number of people had begun to eat cats, which were called "roof rabbits." Many became despondent over the lack of certain types of food. The Germans did not care a bit about the civilians; they kept the best and the most abundant foods for themselves. Many people had begun to die of starvation, and tuberculosis was rampant.

Uncle Henk knew how to get food—he worked secretly with the resistance. The underground movement in Holland had its own methods of stealing food from the Germans, which, of course, had been stolen from the Dutch people to begin with. The Dutch, being quite shrewd, had their ways to fool the Germans on many occasions. Acquiring potatoes was considered a heroic act.

With the extra food that Uncle Henk brought home and the fact that Felix was young, he was soon on the road to recovery.

Dr. Plomp paid another visit to check on Felix and assured us that his illness would not leave any lasting scars. The swelling on his face and body began to slowly disappear.

⊹⊱⊰⊹

September 5, 1944—MAD TUESDAY

September 5, 1944, went down in Dutch history as *Dolle Dinsdag,* meaning "Mad Tuesday." On this day the Allied troops advanced with great speed through northern France and Belgium. This news spread quickly. Parts of the south of Holland had been liberated, and the citizens up north were convinced that the Allied troops would also reach the northern cities the same day.

But the Allied troops had to wait for more supplies in order to be able to push up to the north. This fast-spreading news, combined with the intoxicating feeling of impending liberation among the Dutch, caused the people to lose a sense of reality. Five years of horror, crimes, and persecutions would now come to an end, or so they thought. Dutch flags were raised all over; people went out into the streets screaming, "They are here! They are here! Our liberators are here!" That was a day of mass hysteria.

The hours went by, and no Allied troops were seen in the north. Dreams of a fast liberation went up in smoke. We did not know it then, but we still had to make it through the winter, and the winter of 1944 was to be the worst ever. The Germans resumed their unspeakable atrocities toward the Dutch people by shooting everyone who had Dutch flags raised or who they had suspected were opposed to them. The Germans did not have to answer to anyone, so they shot anyone at random. Premature enthusiasm turned into deadly horror as the worst winter of the war loomed ahead of us.

Then, on September 15, 1944, another unbelievable event took place. Very early in the morning we heard the sound of what we had thought were thousands of Allied airplanes flying overhead. We all ran upstairs to the attic, which had a large window. Looking out, we saw hundreds of paratroopers coming down not far from our home. We became absolutely crazy with excitement. We cried and yelled to each other, "This is it! This is real! They are coming!"

Hannie quickly went to get the hidden crystal radio. All of us wanted to listen, but we did not want to take our eyes off the paratroopers. We learned from the BBC that this was the largest airborne operation ever, dropping three divisions from almost five thousand planes and sliders onto the town of Arnhem to seize bridges in advance of the ground forces. We heard later that, unfortunately, only some of the Allied objectives had been successful. Thousands of men were killed on both sides. All of us took this news very badly, and our hearts went out to the courageous soldiers of the Allied forces.

By now the Dutch people were convinced that the liberation was near. Some people talked about the "German capitulation." However, the resistance papers warned everyone not to be too optimistic and to wait until the Canadians were here. But we heard through the resistance that many in the NSB had fled Holland already. They anticipated their fate when Holland would finally be free.

We wondered about the German occupation forces in Holland. Did they know all that was going on? Would they know that France was free? What about Belgium and the south of Holland?

It seemed that they were unaware because their behavior continued just as sadistically as before.

Nevertheless, all of us were swept away with the thought of freedom. Corrie and I began to get outdoors at night, and we often walked through the meadow enjoying the fresh air. The fighting over our heads went on, and the air raids happened sometimes when we were a distance away from the house. During those times we had to run quickly to the shelter for safety.

There was always a lot of gossip among neighbors when we were in the shelter. Hannie kept us up-to-date on what went on in Holland because he heard the local news from Koen, who still used his boat to load freight.

Then one day near the beginning of October, the best news of all came to us: Piet Brandsen was home. At last our fervent prayers were answered.

+≻=≺+

I was working in the kitchen that day when Aunt Cor ran in; her face was flushed and she was very excited. "Marietje," she uttered breathlessly, "there is a great surprise, and here it is!" She motioned to someone in the hallway, and in came Piet Brandsen.

I let out a big yell, and as I flew into his arms I had to gasp for breath. I could not speak; the emotion was overwhelming. I heard Aunt Cor going up the stairs to get Felix. He came down immediately, and when he saw Piet, he too was overwhelmed. At first, like me, Felix was so stunned he was speechless. Piet looked sickly. He had little color in his face, and he had lost much weight. We could only surmise how he must have suffered at the hands of the Nazis.

We all sat down in the big room, and finally, out came a flood of questions from Felix and me. We had to know everything. Piet told us that he had been released from the camp just a few days before. The Nazis had interrogated him for months; Piet, however, never lost control and stuck to his original story. He told them he had found a copy of *Het Parool* on the train. He denied having anything to do with the resistance. He kept his nerves under control at all times and never once changed his story. We asked him about Piet Kerkhof, the young son of the neighbors of Piet and Dina, whom the Gestapo had arrested at the same time. Piet told us that the Nazis had dismissed him after four months in the camp.

It is difficult to describe our happiness upon Piet's return, especially learning that it was not Felix and I who had precipitated his arrest. Piet told us that Dina and the children had been brave throughout the ordeal. He did not want to discuss the gory details of his time in the camp; in fact, he never disclosed any of these details to anyone after his release.

We spent a long time together that morning. When Aunt Cor left the room Piet, quite emotionally, said to us, "I want to ask the two of you to come back to us and stay until the end of the war. We have gone through thick and thin together, and I don't want to give up now that the end is in sight." We were moved to tears, especially when he added, "Dina and the children want you back too."

Felix and I were deeply touched. My tears began to flow. Piet took our hands in his and said, "Look, think about it. Both Dina and I would like for you to come back. If you want to stay here, then I expect you to come and stay at least a few days with us."

When Piet left, Felix and I went to our room. We did not speak for a long time, and when we finally broke our silence we were filled with emotion. I said, "I hope Piet will gain back his weight; he is not the same Piet anymore."

"That will be impossible," Felix replied. "Without good food it will be very difficult." But we knew that his friends from the resistance would think of a way to secretly provide food for him.

Although we had gained some peace of mind upon Piet's return, none of us was able to relax. The dreaded V-2 missiles launched from sites in our country continued dropping without mercy. We heard on the radio that the city of Antwerp had suffered terrible losses from the rockets, and thousands of people were dead or seriously injured.

Our queen spoke often to the nation, trying to instill hope and pleading for patience. She always poured her heart into her speeches, urging the citizens to remain steadfast. She ended each speech with the words, "May God be with you. Holland shall be free!"

The family kept the crystal radio on all the time. The men took turns listening, and we talked endlessly about the war. We closely followed the news about the United States forces and the Canadian troops, which were making great advances all over. But we realized that we, who lived in the north, had a long wait before the end.

Uncle Henk had a sister who lived with her family on the other side of town. They were nice people who visited often; on occasion they spent the night. Uncle Henk's sister's name was Rika, and her husband's name was Henk. They had two children: a teenage daughter named Greta and a ten-year-old boy named Henkie.

Of course, there had been no choice but for Uncle Henk and Aunt Cor to tell them who we were, so we also called them aunt and uncle.

Piet visited us often, and we could see that it bothered him not to have us in his home. He insisted that we should come for a day. Even when we told him it would be risky for us to leave, he assured us that the Germans were too busy with the way the war was going. Piet had an overpowering personality. He had done much for us; in fact, he had saved our lives and those of Felix's family. I suppose we were drawn under his spell, and finally we could no longer refuse his persuasive requests.

We discussed everything openly with the Hornsvelds. Obviously, they were very surprised, especially since Piet had just been released from a concentration camp. Felix and I did not know what to do. The Hornsvelds pointed out the many dangers in the area. Deep in our own hearts we understood that for Piet, this was a matter of honor, combined with genuine love and friendship for us.

Somehow we lacked the courage to refuse Piet's request. We felt obligated to him for having saved our lives at the darkest and most dangerous period of the persecutions. Finally, after weighing the risks, we gained the reluctant approval of the Hornvelds, and Piet was notified of our upcoming visit.

And so, on a Sunday at six o'clock in the morning we began our trek to the Brandsen home. We left early in the hope of avoiding an encounter with anyone. It was incredibly cold. Our false identity papers were safely tucked in our pockets. Felix wore his uniform with the postal insignias attached. I was quite nervous, and I kept looking behind me to see if anyone was following us. Felix, however, did not display any fear.

We walked calmly, acting as if this was our daily exercise. Felix and I had carefully discussed the various possibilities that could take place as we made our way to the Brandsens'. For instance, we decided that if an air raid took place, we would not go into anyone's home. And if a German stopped us, Felix would speak in German and react carefully, according to the situation.

We made it through the inlet without meeting any German soldiers; all was well. Finally we came to Piet's street, and after entering the notorious alley, I let out a sigh of relief; at last the first part of this mad undertaking was over. But as Felix and I walked through Piet's backyard, the memories of the night of terror, when Piet was arrested by the Gestapo, began to haunt me, and I began to doubt the wisdom of our visit.

The Brandsen family was waiting for us. What a reunion it was! The children were adorable; they did not want to let go of us; they clung so tightly. There was so much to talk about. We asked about Opa, the neighbors, and how Piet Kerkhoff had fared in that horrible concentration camp. We talked about the Van den Hoeven family, about Felix's family, and how Kurt's mother was holding up, especially with her diabetes. For hours we discussed the course of the war and the food rations.

Piet had arranged with the Van den Hoevens for Kurt to come to the Brandsen home around dusk. The Van den Hoeven family was very reluctant for us to come to their home, which we understood quite well.

Aside from the air raids, for which we did not run into the shelter, the day went by too quickly and too pleasantly. But as dusk began to set in, I became edgy and hoped that Kurt would come quickly. Indeed, within minutes after dusk he entered through the kitchen. As we embraced he said, "Our mothers are holding up well. Nel is okay, but the food is a big problem. We will manage the best we can," he added with a worrisome look on his face.

It seemed to me that the conversation went on endlessly, and I began to remind everyone that we had to leave and make our way back. The Brandsens wanted us to spend the night, but we politely declined; we knew the Hornsvelds would worry. We had to be back before curfew.

As Kurt left, Felix and I also parted with many hugs and kisses. Dina and the children made the sign of the cross as we left and wished us Godspeed along our way. Walking from the alley to the street, I once again became overwhelmed with that ominous feeling of fear. Darkness had set in. It was difficult to see where we were going. But we recognized the canals, and just as we detected the vague outlines of the ancient castle that we had to pass that led to the inlet, my ominous feelings turned into reality.

Before me was my nightmare: a German sentry standing guard. He approached us and, shining his flashlight on us, yelled, "Halt!" As he came nearer, he shouted in German, "Who are you? Where are you going?" My heart began to pound, and my body began to shake. The soldier looked suspiciously at Felix's uniform, and I saw by the expression on his face that he wondered what profession Felix was in.

Luckily Felix was well prepared. The soldier's uniform did not have the dreaded Gestapo or SS insignias on it, and Felix began to speak to him in German, his native tongue. In a brusque tone of voice, Felix said with unbelievable confidence, "What do you mean? We live right here on a boat; we are out on our evening walk." The German looked around a bit, but I believe, on account of the dark, he could not see much. Only Koen's boat was there.

Then Felix said sternly, "Look, we have to get through, and if you don't let us in, I will report it to your superior." The man must have been mightily impressed with Felix, and upon hearing the word *superior,* he let us go. Of all things, he clicked his heels, saluted, and disappeared into the dark.

It was an unforgettable experience. When we were safely back with the Hornsvelds we told them our story. It taught all of us a lesson not to act prematurely. The war was still raging on, and all of us had a long, long way to go.

CHAPTER 13

The Road to Freedom

Mr. and Mrs. Van den Hoeven

One evening when the Brandt family was visiting, Hannie stormed into the room. Looking at his father, he shouted in an excited voice, "Pa, guess what happened? The Germans have stolen all the cars out of the crate factory, and they have filled it up with grain. The whole building is overflowing with grain." We were stunned by this news. The cars belonged to private citizens who had hidden them in the empty factory, thinking the vehicles would be safe there.

Henk asked, "How do you know?"

"From Koen," Hannie continued, swallowing hard from excitement. "He saw the whole thing. The *Moffen* have stolen everything from the farmers, and we must do something about it." Turning to Bertus, he pleaded, "Bert, you have to help, and we must do something before the *Moffen* take the grain to Germany. It is a must."

Henk, as always, did not react at first; he was deep in thought. We all knew we had come to the point where the surrogate food was inedible. The farmers also were at their last resources with most of their livestock gone. Finally after a long silence, Henk said, "However do you think that we can pull anything off without being caught?"

Hannie, with great confidence and youthful vigor, replied, "I will think of something. We must come up with a plan; we must fool the *Moffen*."

Uncle Henk's office staff was gone, and we had more freedom now. Instead of addressing our hosts as aunt and uncle, we found it was easier and shorter to call them "Moe" and "Pa."

A few days later Hannie announced that he had a great idea. He spoke with much enthusiasm. "Listen, I have it all worked out," he said. "We must dig a tunnel and then get to the inside of the factory and get to the grain."

No one said a word at first. But then Bertus spoke. "I think we can pull it off," he said, "if we do it during the night."

I could see that Pa was hesitant. Finally after much discussion, the decision was made, mostly because of the scarcity of food and the prospect of a long winter ahead. And thus, with the okay from Pa, the boys prepared themselves for this daring adventure.

The next evening, assisted by their Uncle Henk Brandt, they began to work on digging a tunnel. Each night when they returned home safely, we sighed in relief. After a week had gone by, they triumphantly announced that the tunnel was ready. They had found a way to connect the tunnel to the factory, and they were set to go.

Now we had to work on all of the details of who should go through, what time of night, how to get the grain out, and who should be on the lookout for Germans. It was decided that Corrie should stand guard. Each night we talked and talked, until all of us were completely swept up in the enthusiasm. Felix and I immediately volunteered to come along with the Hornsveld family into the tunnel. The Brandt family would also join in. Koen had given Hannie a large supply of cloth sacks; in turn, Hannie promised to give him part of the grain. Koen had added, "I hope you will be successful; I'll keep an eye out for you." Uncle Henk, now quite emotionally involved in the plan, said jokingly, "What the heck, let's take as much as we can from the *Rot-Moffen*."

The next night when it was very late, all of us sneaked out toward the tunnel, each holding a cloth sack. It was pitch-dark and very cold, but we could not wear heavy clothes; we needed to fit in the narrow tunnel. We crawled through the tunnel, and when the last of us had reached the inside of the factory, we fell down in the middle of the grain. The tension had been awesome. We could not see a thing; we could only feel the grain around us. It was so dusty that Aunt Rika began to sneeze incessantly. Her husband had to hold his hand over her face the whole time. After a short rest we began to fill up the sacks, using our hands. It took a very long time.

Each time we thought we heard something, we hid under the grain. It must have been mice running around. It seemed like an eternity before our mission was over; we were in there for a long time, always on alert for possible dangers. Finally, after hours had gone by and we had filled the sacks, we had to crawl out of the tunnel, toting the very heavy sacks behind us. Going into the tunnel with empty sacks was nothing compared to our journey back with the very heavy loads. By then it was three o'clock in the morning. We found little Corrie bravely standing guard. We reached the house safely, worn out, excited, tired, but happy. There was now enough food to last for a while. Of course we shared our grain with the Van den Hoevens, and Koen got his share as well.

Perhaps because we were not used to eating the heavy grain, or perhaps because of the excitement, Felix and I became quite sick with dysentery. We both had high fevers, but we refused to have a doctor come to the house. Aunt Cor, who was quite concerned, had us use several old Dutch folk remedies, which seemed to help because slowly we began to recuperate, although the illness left us weak for a long time.

The winter of 1944 was the worst that I can remember. Because we knew that part of southern Holland was free, our hopes had been raised for liberation. It was not yet to be. In December the Allies—before they could cross the Rhine River—had to face a last-stand German onslaught in the Ardennes Forest. It came as a complete surprise for the Allies. The Battle of the Bulge, as it was called, had begun.

We listened day and night to the BBC. Felix, meanwhile, wrote feverishly in his diary—it was now many, many pages, all written in pencil. I often said, "How senseless is war; everyone loses; all those young lives are snuffed out because of the Germans and their crazy

Führer." I asked why this horrible fight was called the Battle of the Bulge, and Felix explained that the bulging shape of the battleground could be seen on the map. As a matter of fact, the Hornsvelds, Felix, and I looked at an old atlas, and in our minds we followed the Allied troops, trying to figure out where they were, how the war progressed, and when it would all be over.

Christmas came and went. It was the sixth one for us in this endless war. My thoughts returned to December of 1939, when I was in England helping Miss Morling with the Christmas decorations while thinking with sadness of the Hanukkah festivities of my youth. Was Miss Morling still alive? What about all of my family and friends in Rotterdam? I became quite melancholy, and I could not wait for December to be over.

The Germans grew more and more frantic. Their ordinances had become even more nonsensical; one of them instructed people to turn in metal doorknobs, metal handles from furniture, metal housewares, garden tools, and other metal items. Of course, the ordinance was accompanied by the usual threats.

The river was frozen stiff. Since I had my fake identity papers, and I was the "niece" of the family, I often went skating with Corrie, usually at dusk. For a short while I could divert my mind and dream of being free.

And finally, December was gone and the new year of 1945 began. What would it bring? Would we spend another year in hiding? It seemed like an eternity of waiting and hoping. The grain was helping us all to endure and stay alive. And so we kept praying that the Almighty would fulfill the wishes of our hearts.

+=+=+

Around the first week in February, Pa and Moe told us that they wanted to go away for one day to visit their family in Amsterdam, whom they had not seen for several years. They asked us if we could manage by ourselves. We courageously said, "Yes, of course," although deep in my heart I was worried. Of course I was happy for them that they would get to see their loved ones after all that had transpired. Felix emphasized that they should not be concerned about us and that we would be fine.

Pa said, "You know, I heard through the grapevine"—he always used the term *grapevine*, he never mentioned the resistance— "that the SS and the Gestapo in the office across the river have taken to their heels. But still," he continued, "stay on your guard just the same."

That Sunday morning the entire family left: Pa, Moe, Hannie, Bert, and Corrie. The big house felt totally abandoned. Another concern was that we did not know the neighbors. That is, they said hello when we were together in the air raid shelter; they seemed to tolerate us, but they never asked questions or spoke to us. I had found it strange to meet those people, and I never knew exactly who they were.

Felix said, "Let's stay upstairs. If something happens, then we are close to our hiding place." I agreed. The big window in the attic gave us ample chance to view the area. A few hours went by. Felix was writing and I was dozing off when we heard a noise. I ran to the window and suddenly saw two Germans going around the house. I motioned to Felix, who immediately went into his hiding cell in the floor. I quickly threw a rug over the cell, and in a dream-state I went down the steps and into the kitchen.

After a few minutes the Germans began battering on the door. What to do? My brain began to work overtime. If I did not answer, they might kick the door in. I was left but one choice: open the door. I quickly ran to the front door, opened it, stepped out, and quickly closed it behind me.

There I was, face-to-face with the two Germans. I hastily looked at their uniforms. There were no dreaded SS or Gestapo insignias on them. They were ordinary German soldiers. One of them was very tall. If he had not been the enemy, I would have classified him as handsome. The shorter one looked a bit dumb. I did not like the way that the tall one looked at me. He lifted his hand to his cap politely and said, "We need horses; are there any around here? Where are they?"

I nodded and quickly put on my wooden shoes, which stood outside the door. I started to walk toward the meadow that was situated beyond the body of water; the two Germans were following me from behind. I could understand what they were saying while they were talking to each other. I heard them comment about my wooden shoes; the shoes prevented me from walking as fast as I would have liked to. I was shivering badly, both from emotional turmoil and from the cold. In my haste I had forgotten to take my coat.

I finally reached the meadow where I knew the horses were. One of them looked old and quite exhausted. I did not know who the owner of the horses was, but to get rid of the Germans I told the two soldiers to go ahead and take them. The two men talked awhile between themselves, the tall one all the time looking at me in a flirtatious manner. Silently, I prayed very hard that they would go away and leave me alone. Finally, they slowly walked to the horses, and each of them took one. The tall one clicked his heels and saluted, and then the two of them disappeared through a path back beyond the meadow. The entire episode was bizarre. Had they only known they had saluted a Jewish girl.

When they were out of sight, I ran toward the house and up the stairs to the attic and called out to Felix to come out of the hiding place. I told him what had happened. He had been terribly worried, especially because I had been gone for such a long time.

When the Hornsvelds returned, we were overjoyed to have the family back again. We waited awhile before telling them what had transpired while they were gone. I said, "I saw no other way out but to let them have the horses."

Pa answered, "What the heck, don't worry, you did the right thing. I know who the horses belong to. But there is not enough food for them anyway. The *Moffen* can feed them better than we can." Pa added, as he looked at my guilt-stricken face, "It's only the horses. Let's be glad it was not you." And with that, the incident was closed.

Around that time I noticed that Moe was cooking much more than usual. I did not ask any questions. But one day Hannie came over to us and said, "Have you noticed that Moe is cooking all of the time?"

"Yes," I answered, "but I don't know why."

"I will tell you, but it is strictly confidential," he said.

Hannie, Felix, and I went upstairs where we could be alone, and when we sat down we could hardly wait for Hannie to start talking.

Without any prelude he said, "Moe is cooking for the paratroopers."

Felix and I asked, "What paratroopers?"

"Pa and some others rescued nineteen paratroopers; they are hidden behind the dockyard." Our mouths fell open in surprise. "Yes," Hannie continued. "We are getting fisherman's outfits for them; then they will be transported to the coast." Hannie apparently relished in our astonishment, and we could tell that he was happy to tell us about it, knowing the secret was safe with us.

I asked naively, "Who will pick them up?"

"Don't you know that Holland has secret connections with the Allies?" he asked. "Especially with England." He continued with much gusto, "All will be over soon—the resistance is being supplied with lots of weapons. The Allies are dropping them off at secret places here in Holland, and when our liberators come, then we Dutch can help them with all of our weapons."

Pa and Moe and Bertus would never openly discuss these things. But we were grateful to Hannie for confiding in us; it gave us a big boost. We asked him, "How will the paratroopers get to the coast, and where will they be dropped off?"

"I know about the general plan but not the details," he answered. "Usually somewhere near Scheveningen at secret places. The resistance has radio contact with the Allies. They know that we Dutch are reliable and that we can be trusted." As Hannie left, he placed his finger over his lips and whispered, "They know that we can keep our mouths shut."

After he was gone, I said to Felix, "Well, well, well! Things sure look better now. I feel truly encouraged." Felix, down to earth as always, admonished me by saying, "We are not there yet; much can still happen. But," he added, "things do look much better."

And indeed, that same night we heard on the crystal all of the important events that were taking place. The Allies had cleared the west bank of the De Roer River, and they had captured the city of Cologne. Our joy overtook the fear we had for the Germans, who kept bragging—against reality—about their imaginary victories.

Just a few days later, at six o'clock in the morning, all of us in the house were awakened by the sound of a voice through a loudspeaker. It was a German shouting, "All men in the family must come forward and report." He repeated these words over and over. Pa came running in his pajamas to the attic, where Bertus and Felix were sleeping. With an alarmed look on his face, he uttered, "Hey, boys, can you hear it? There is a *rot-mof* downstairs. What should we do?"

Felix got up and, looking through the window, said with a stern tone, "We must do nothing! The end of the war is near, and we are not giving up now. Let's just ignore it."

As the soldier walked farther down through the area, his shouting faded away in the distance. Apparently, no one in the neighborhood paid any attention. Soon the whole ordeal was over. But to be on the safe side, the boys stayed put inside the house. My ice skating with Corrie ended also. We all pledged to be extra careful, especially because we felt that freedom was near.

Later that month we learned that Himmler, the butcher of Europe, had tried to negotiate peace with Great Britain and the United States. But the Allies demanded that all German troops surrender on all fronts.

The month of March started with good news about the war. Finland declared war on Germany, and the Russian armies swept into eastern Hungary. They joined forces with Yugoslavia, swinging north and capturing Vienna and eastern Austria. The Red Army crashed into Warsaw and Kraków.

Felix continued to write fervently in his diary, leaving out no details. The news about the war became so exciting that people in Holland grew bolder by the day. Secrets that could never have been told before now came to light. The Dutch, known for their restrained and somewhat sober nature—not sensationalistic—now came out of their shell. They talked openly, and there seemed to be no holding back.

Around the third week in March Piet came to see us, as he did from time to time. Although I was upstairs, I recognized his voice immediately, and when I came down I saw him talking to Pa in the hallway. I detected a tone of excitement in their voices as Pa called out to me, "Marietje, go and get Jan. We have great news for you."

In the excitement of the moment, I naively thought that they had found my mother. I ran up the stairs to get Felix. I shouted, "Come quick, there is great news!" I threw my hands up in the air, mumbling incoherently, "What can it be? Oh God, please let it be my mother..."

When we entered the large room, Moe was also there. Piet looked at me with that special gleam in his eye that I knew so well. As he put his pipe in the ashtray, he took my hands in his and said, "I found your brother Ies and his wife."

I could not absorb this incredible news at first. My mouth fell open. I managed to ask, "Where are they? Are they all right? What happened?"

Piet, always under control, said calmly, "They are not well. The people with whom they have been hiding are completely out of food. They cannot possibly shelter them any longer."

As Piet continued smoking his pipe, I lamented, "Goodness, can we see them? And what about my sister and her husband?" I continued to jabber, looking from one person to another. Felix held me tight, trying to calm me down.

Pa said, "Piet will tell us everything, and then we can see if there is anything we can do to help." I sat down, pretending to be calm, as Piet began to talk.

"I heard from friends of the neighbors that your brother and his wife are hiding with the family Veenhuizen on Het Havik, right near here," he said. We knew where Het Havik was. Of all things, on that notorious day of our visit to the Brandsens, we must have passed the very house.

Piet continued, "Your family is not well and we must move them." He then divulged that Ies and Bep were hidden in a small space in the attic and that the family needed a ladder to get them food after opening a trapdoor. As for using the bathroom, my brother and his wife had to knock and wait for someone to come with a ladder to let them out. They had not been out of this hole for all of these years.

Moe, being the wonderfully practical person that she was, said, "The first thing we have to do is get food to them. I'll tell Corrie to bring it there." Moe then motioned to me. "Come on, Marietje, let's go to the kitchen. In the meantime, let them decide what should be done next." In the kitchen Moe selected some nourishing food items, and we began to cook a meal. When the food was ready,

Moe handed me a large tin. She said, "Try to get everything in while I get Corrie ready and tell her where to go and what to say."

When Corrie came into the room, she was already wrapped in warm clothes, holding the large can. Piet gave her the exact address and instructed her as to what to say. I had wanted to write a letter to my brother to accompany the food, but they all advised me against it. Corrie was instructed to ring the doorbell and say, "Here is food for you and for the family upstairs, from their sister." She was not to divulge who she was or where she lived.

As Corrie left, Piet said in his colorful way, "I'll be damned if a lot of Germans are not already out of here. They must know that the Canadians are pulling up to the north. Every person who has his head together knows by now that it won't be long until the *Moffen* are gone."

As he began to smoke his pipe again, in walked the Brandt family. They had come regularly to pick up wheat, which the boys continued to courageously take through the tunnel during the night.

All of us were now in the room, talking excitedly about the incoming troops. The conversation then shifted to the news about my brother and his wife. Piet repeated everything to the Brandt family. They listened attentively and shook their heads in sympathy, all the while looking at Felix and me.

Suddenly Aunt Rika turned to her husband with a pleading look on her face and said, "Henk, can't we take them in? We can make room for them upstairs."

Uncle Henk did not hesitate for one moment and replied, nodding to his wife, "No problem at all. It is fine with me. We have to help those poor people. Imagine living in a hole for all that time."

It was a moment never to be forgotten; how lucky we were to encounter such generous, altruistic people whenever a crisis arose!

We waited for Corrie to come back, and when she finally returned we wanted to know exactly what had happened. She calmly said, "It went fine. After I rang the bell, a woman opened the door and I said what you told me to say. There was nothing to it. She took the can and thanked me. I'm sure she understood what it was all about."

We were elated that everything had gone well. I gave Corrie a big hug, and Felix and I thanked everyone from the depths of our hearts. As we all got up to leave, Piet said, "Henk and I will work something out, and I promise you that it will be soon."

Through Pa and the Van den Hoeven family, we had continued to maintain some regular contact with Felix's family. But this situation with my brother was different; although we knew my family members had been found, we could not contact them or see them. We just had to be patient, to wait, and to trust in fate.

After a few days had passed with Corrie regularly taking food to the home on Het Havik, Pa said to us, "It is time to take your family to Rika and Henk. They are ready for them. I discussed everything with Piet—how to go about getting them there safely."

I had been pondering when my brother and his wife would go to Henk and Rika's. How would things work out? Would they be safe? I tried hard to maintain my composure at all times, careful not to reveal my anxiety. I couldn't help but remember my excitement, my fears, and my hopes when Piet was to take my mother to a safe hiding place and how desperate I became when things went wrong. I had never gotten over that tragedy, and I knew that for the rest of my life I never would.

But at the end of that week, just as I had calmed down, both Felix and I were upstairs when Pa came into the room. He had a look on his face that seemed to say something good had occurred. As he sat down on the bed, he said with no preamble, "Your brother and his wife are now safe with Henk and Rika."

I stared at him, at first not believing that all had gone so well. Then I went over to him and hugged him tightly. The questions then tumbled out of my mouth, "How, when, how are they … ?"

He said, "Take it easy; they are fine now. I went last night to the family on Het Havik. I told them that I knew about the hiding of Ies and Bep and that I knew of another place for them. The family was agreeable; they trusted me. They got your brother and his wife down the ladder. I put them at ease, and we walked slowly to Rika and Henk's home, where they are now safe." Pa made it all sound so easy, although in our hearts we knew that it must have been a dangerous and complicated ordeal.

I asked, "How do they look and are they okay?" Pa winked his eye and said in a typical understated Dutch way, "Well, they don't look as if they came from a spa, but I can assure you that they will be all right again." And with that, he left our room.

Felix consoled me as I began to cry. He took me in his arms and said, "Let's be grateful for these wonderful people; we must pray that the Almighty will continue to bestow his blessings on them." We sat there in that small room for a long time in complete silence, both absorbed in our own thoughts, yet both thinking the same thing: when would it finally be over?

CHAPTER 14

The End of the Road

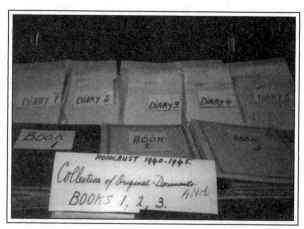

*Felix's five diaries and my three books with
hundreds of documents about the Holocaust*

In April 1945 confusion and tension grew by the day. The crystal
radio was so full of news from all the events taking place, one after
the other, that it was almost impossible to keep up with everything.

We needed to get rid of the Germans as soon as possible or we
would all die of starvation. Food rations had been minimized to half a
loaf of bread per person per week, along with a small portion of meat.

We counted ourselves lucky to have some wheat left. It had become
impossible for the boys to go through the tunnel any longer because
lately we had seen a great number of German soldiers in our area.

On April 12, 1945, we were shocked to hear the sad news on the
crystal radio that the American president, Franklin D. Roosevelt, had

died. Pa said, "What a blow … I feel as if it were a personal loss that this had to happen just now." Our joy over the impending liberation was severely tempered.

Later that week we heard loud shooting outside. We dressed quickly and came together in the large room. Looking out the window, we saw a great number of German soldiers running toward the house. They began to bang on the door and yell loudly. At first we all huddled together in fear for our lives. Finally Pa went and opened the front door. A German officer screamed, "Aus, aus, Alle muessen heraus, schnell, schnell!" Translated, this means, "Out, out, everybody must go out, quick, quick!"

We all ran into the air raid shelter amid the heavy shooting, which was taking place right over our heads. It turned out that the Canadians were already in the area, on one side of the river, shooting at the Germans, who were on the other side. The noise was deafening with planes flying low. The end was so near, and yet we wondered, would we be able to survive?

Amid the chaos, we could not quite figure out what was going on. The firing at times tapered, and during those times, if we did not see any Germans, we ran back to the house to fetch some food and personal belongings. We realized that we had to stay in the air raid shelter as we heard the Germans shouting and yelling nervously at the top of their lungs. The time dragged on slowly as we contemplated what we should do.

Night came, and we realized that there was nothing for us to do but stay in the shelter. Sometimes, as we sat leaning against each other, a few of us would lie down. Occasionally Hannie stuck his head out the entrance to survey the situation. Each time he came back down, he reported that the Germans were still nearby. By this time hunger pangs had set in. Corrie moaned, "Moe, I am hungry." It had been a full day and night that we had been cooped up in the shelter.

The next morning, as dawn broke, Hannie suddenly turned to Pa and Bertus, and with a look of expectation in his eyes he said, "Pa, we might have a way out. Do you remember the circus wagon that belongs to Hammersen and Vermolen? It is still stored away down beyond the dockyard."

Pa nodded slowly and said, "What about it?"

"Well," continued Hannie, "I remember that Bakker's helper told me that he still takes care of that old horse nearby in the barn. We cannot possibly survive in this hole here, and who knows how long this will go on? Let's try to take the wagon and the horse and get out of here."

Pa carefully thought through the idea. After all, he had the responsibility for his family and for Felix and me. Moe and Bertus remarked, "What, for heaven's sake, are we to do? We cannot possibly stay here. One way or the other, our lives are at stake."

Bertus added with a tone of urgency, "Yes, Pa, it is our last chance. The Canadians are here already."

Pa, still pondering this dangerous idea, said to no one in particular, "Where can we go with that old horse?"

Moe answered, "Well, all I can think of is going to Rika and Henk." We knew they lived at the opposite end of our town, quite far from where we were.

The conversation continued back and forth as we considered the pros and cons of taking the circus truck and the horse. Then Felix said, "We must take a chance; it is the only hope for survival. We are in the midst of a battle. The Germans are very nervous, and they might kill us and no one would know. We have to find a way out."

Finally, we all agreed to do everything possible to escape from the dreaded air raid shelter. Hannie and Bertus were ready to get to work immediately. Felix said, "Please let me go with you. I know all about horses; I was raised on a farm."

But Pa, the fear of hiding still fresh in his mind, said, "Jan, you better stay with us for now; you can help later."

And so the two boys left the shelter amid the fighting, leaving the rest of us in a terrific state of fear. We were on pins and needles; I prayed silently, asking God for their safe return. We pretended to be calm, but our thoughts were spinning wildly. The waiting seemed to last an eternity; no one spoke a word. Just as Felix mentioned, "I'll go and see what's going on," the boys returned to the shelter.

They shouted excitedly over the tumult, "We got the wagon and the horse. Come quickly!" Hannie shouted, "We had a darned job to get the horse ready and getting the harness over his head."

We ran through the lumberyard, and indeed, there it was: the circus wagon and the old horse hitched in front of the carriage. We stepped in quickly while the Germans and Canadians were shooting at each other across the river. Felix took the horse by the reins, trying to calm it down. Amid the fury of the fighting, we left in the direction of the Brandt home, with Felix leading the horse as he walked beside the wagon.

The horse trotted very slowly, afraid of the noise and not used to being out. It often pulled its ears down, not wanting to continue on.

We used back roads to avoid the fighting. It was a long, long trip—it seemed as if it would never end.

Finally we reached the home of the Brandt family. We rang the bell, and when they answered the door they were flabbergasted to see us step out of a circus wagon and into their home.

Aunt Rika threw up her hands into the air and shouted, "Oh, my God, oh, my goodness, what's happened! Come in, come in!"

Her husband took it more calmly. He said, "Sit down, sit down, let's hear what happened." Turning to his wife, he said, "Rika, get Ies and Bep here; boy, oh, boy, will they ever be surprised to see their family here!"

After a few minutes my brother and his wife came into the room. My heart began to pound. I was elated beyond words to be reunited with my oldest brother and my sister-in-law. The years of slaughter, persecutions, and hiding had left their mark on them. I noticed in a flash how unwell they looked, so aged and ailing. But then we flew into each other's arms, crying and laughing at the same time. We hugged and kissed and could not speak for a while.

As the emotion of the moment began to calm a little, Aunt Rika said, "You all look downright exhausted and beat up, but we are dying to know what happened."

After we were settled in, Pa began to relate the story of our escape and how the boys courageously had gone to the dockyard to get the circus wagon and the old horse. He told of our flight—our painfully slow one—amid the fierce battle. The more Pa talked, the more we realized how we had gambled with our lives in a desperate bid for survival and freedom.

Another miracle had taken place. All we could do now was wait for the end of this miserable war.

It is difficult to believe that thirteen people managed to live in the small home of the Brandt family. The greatest part of that time was spent near the crystal radio, which was hidden upstairs. Some of us slept on the floor, or we slept together in a bed. Some of us kept our ears glued to the crystal radio, not wanting to miss a minute of the news, which continued to be broadcast day and night. I shared a bed with the Brandt children, and we slept with our clothes on. The airplanes were flying so low we could almost see the pilots. Pa said, "Don't worry, these are Allied planes; they are throwing weapons out."

Around the end of April Felix and Pa came running into the bedroom. Felix managed to say, "Listen to this! The Italian partisans have captured Mussolini. They have shot him and his mistress somewhere in northern Italy."

Pa added, catching his breath, "Boy, oh, boy, and the Russian units are already on the Elbe River." There was so much good news that we were upbeat. There was hardly time to prepare food. The incredible events reported in the news overtook everything, even our hunger pangs.

The climax came on April 30, 1945. I was dozing off with some of the women as the men came in screaming at us to wake up. They yelled, "Hitler and his mistress Eva Braun are dead!"

Henk Brandt, with his hand waving in the air, began to dance around, screaming, "Finally, finally, we will get rid of those bastards!"

None of us could sleep that night. When we calmed down a bit, we learned that Hitler and Eva Braun had committed suicide. Of course, the Germans still denied it. They maintained that Hitler had died defending Berlin and that he had named Admiral Karl Doenitz as his successor. The BBC confirmed that after the suicide their bodies had been burned.

In the excitement of all this good news, the family wanted to raise the Dutch flag, but there were warnings on the radio not to be too hasty and to stay inside our homes for safety. The tension was enormous throughout Holland; it built by the hour.

One of Pa's friends from the resistance came to our home the next day. He told us that they were preparing to arrest members of the NSB, especially the NSB mayor of Amersfoort. They were only waiting for the Canadians to come in. But the Germans did not give up. When they were told that they had to capitulate, the German commandant maintained that the rumors were false and that it was only *Waffen Ruhe* (Armistice).

Then on Friday night, May 4, 1945, we heard people running jubilantly in the streets, yelling, "There is peace, peace; the surrender goes in tomorrow morning!" We ran to listen to the radio because we weren't sure if it was true. After all, the curfew was still on. Or was it? It seemed as if nobody thought any longer of the so-called *Sperr Stunden*, that horrible German word for curfew hours.

However, our joy did not last long. At eleven o'clock that night the Germans came unexpectedly, shooting their way through the streets. All of us dashed inside, totally confused and appalled at the same time. In no time the streets were again silent.

The next day, Saturday, May 5, uncertainty got the better of us. The radio announced that we had to wait for the Allied troops to come in. The German military was still standing guard. The SS police still occupied bridges, were still arresting citizens, and seemed to still be shooting as much as they wished. Uncle Henk said, "Aren't the *Moffen* ever going to give up? What poor losers!"

And so it went: our expectations dashed once more. It was clear that the Germans themselves did not know what was going on. One group of their armed forces seemed to know that they had to give up, and another group claimed that there was only an armistice.

Suddenly, late that night, Bertus, Hannie, and Felix came running down the stairs, gesturing wildly and stumbling over their words, shouting, "There is unconditional surrender! The Germans have surrendered!" We became hysterical. As others came down the stairs, we hugged them, they hugged us, we kissed them, they kissed us, we cried, we screamed, we fell over each other. I cannot fully describe that eventful, glorious night.

Amid the screaming and the yelling, Felix took me into his arms. While we embraced, he uttered over and over again, with tears streaming down his face, "We made it, we made it, thank God we made it." We stood there for a while, trying to realize that we were truly free.

Then Uncle Henk Brandt left the room. After a while he returned carrying two bottles of Dutch gin. As he smiled broadly, he said, "Let's have a good one and get drunk! I hid these two bottles and saved them all these darned years just for this occasion." Despite our empty stomachs, we drank "a good one." I lost my balance and fell under the table, but it was worth it.

Then we went upstairs to listen to the small crystal radio that had served us well on so many occasions and saved us from desperation and thoughts of giving up. We learned that on Monday, May 7, 1945, German General Alfred Jodl of the German High Command had entered the Allied headquarters in Reims, France, and there in a red school building had signed the terms of the unconditional surrender on behalf of his government. General Eisenhower's chief of staff, General Walter Smith, had signed for the Allies.

On May 9, 1945, Berlin ratified the surrender terms. After five years and eight months, the European phase of this horrible war had ended. My country, the Netherlands, was liberated by the Canadians under General Henry Crerar, and on May 9 the word went forth: *Holland is free!*

The Dutch authorities immediately issued an ordinance admonishing the Germans not to shoot while leaving and saying that if they did continue to shoot weapons at the Dutch civilians, they would be considered war criminals and arrested. Shortly thereafter Queen Wilhelmina, her daughter, Juliana, and her husband, Prince Bernhard, along with their three children returned to Holland.

For us, the next phase was to figure out where to go, what to do, and how to find the rest of our family members.

+━━+

We had not seen any Canadians in our area, and we very much wanted to go out into the streets. But it was already near midnight, and Pa said, "Listen, all of us desperately need some rest. Let's try to get some sleep and leave early tomorrow morning."

Moe agreed with him. She added, "We must go and see if our house is still there. And you, Jan and Marietje, have to go to the Van den Hoevens' and get together with your family, while Bep and Ies have to go to see about their store."

Aunt Rika nodded in agreement. She remarked, "I know that none of us can sleep, but we must at least rest for a few hours and gather some strength."

They were right. All of us felt emotionally and physically drained. We were too tired to even take off our clothes, and we fell down wherever there was room. Early the next morning we went out into the street. We still could not believe that we were free. As we saw the Germans leaving, a lot of people shouted obscenities at them. Some Dutch people even wanted to get into physical fights with the Germans. The Hornsveld family left at the same time we did, and then Felix, Ies, Bep, and I were on our way. We planned to first go to the Van den Hoevens' and see Felix's family.

Suddenly we heard from far off a dull, droning sound. The sound came closer and closer. Our first reaction was, "Seek shelter!" But then we saw hundreds of people standing on the rooftops of houses, cheering wildly and shouting with joy, waving at the airplanes. Felix took a good look and shouted over the noise, "Oh, my word, they are Lancasters! They are throwing food items from the planes."

Now we could clearly see the planes soaring stately over the neighboring towns and villages. The people became almost hysterical. They wanted to know where the food was—food that we had all needed for so long. Then some organizers called out that we had to wait just a while longer until the food could be properly distributed.

Winding our way through the throngs of people, we finally reached the Van den Hoeven home. At that point we were only in fair condition, but at least we were alive. When we entered the house, Felix's mother was clutching her prayer book in her hand; Mrs. Van den Hoeven said, "Your mother would not let go of it all of these years."

We stayed there for quite a while, but my brother was eager to go to his store. And so the four of us took off again. On our way we passed thousands of people dancing in the streets, some of them singing our national anthem, "Het Wilhelmus." At times we stood still and joined in. It was all very moving, almost surreal. Flags were waving all over: British flags, American flags, Canadian flags, and of course Dutch flags. Everyone wore orange ribbons, orange shawls, orange buttons; the color orange was the Dutch national symbol of the House of Orange. There was even a man on the street handing out flyers with the words to the American national anthem, neatly typed in English, with the Dutch translation typed underneath. I wondered how he had gotten them.

It took a long, long time to push our way through the enthusiastic crowds. But finally we reached the street we were looking for, called Het Hof. Lo and behold, the store was still there, albeit changed on both the inside and the outside.

The next thing we knew, a man who owned the business next to my brother's appeared; I remembered him well from before the war. His name was Mr. Veenendaal. He ran over to Ies and gave him a huge, heart-filled bear hug. He then embraced the rest of us.

This neighbor used to run an art shop next to my brother's delicatessen. He said to us, "Let me get some chairs; we'll sit and I'll tell you what happened." After we were seated, he began to explain how he had fooled the Germans by wallpapering the entire store. He had taken out all of my brother's equipment and stored it away, replacing the equipment with his own art materials.

He finished his story and turned to my brother and said, "You know, Cohen, I am a good Christian and I prayed every day that somehow, someday, you'd come back. Thanks to the good Lord, by golly, here you are. Welcome back." While my brother wiped the tears from his eyes, my sister-in-law and I began to cry. We were moved by this man's concern and caring for my brother.

As we were still talking with this neighbor, the miracles continued. Even the most well-made movie with a powerful ending could not compare to this.

The five of us were so wrapped up in our conversation that we did not see two more people approaching. But then my heart began to pound as I turned and saw my sister and her husband; they seemed to appear out of nowhere. I saw at a glance how terribly sick my sister's husband looked. While my sister did not look too bad, I noticed that she had lost a lot of weight and her beauty was gone.

But what a reunion it was! We flew into each other's arms, our emotions soaring, the words tumbling out of our mouths as we asked questions. We wanted to know everything all at once from one another. Finally, I learned that they had found shelter with a farming family in Hoogland, a neighboring village. They had spent their days and nights in a loft in the barn, sleeping with the cows and horses.

We were all talking animatedly. I then noticed a young man dressed in a military uniform coming around the corner of the street and walking slowly toward us. There was something familiar in his step, and I thought to myself, "He looks like my brother Ben; but no, that cannot be." I thought I was delusional, the effects of many years of hiding. As this young man came closer, I became convinced that in all of the excitement I had lost my mind. He looked so much like Ben.

Then my sister ran to him, screaming, "It is Ben; oh, my God, it is Ben! Ben is back, Ben, Ben, oh, Ben!"

I stood there, immobilized, thinking, "Am I dreaming?"

The neighbor came with some water, and my brother embraced me. Ies repeated over and over, "How is it possible? Where were you all of these years? With what units … in what army?" He went on and on with the same questions. After I gained my sense of reality, I noticed how handsome my brother looked in his colorful uniform, which was decorated with a number of medals.

Mr. Veenendaal seemed to fully understand our emotional state. He said, "This I want to hear. I must hear what happened." Then several more people came over to where we were standing, and in no time a small crowd had assembled to find out who this military man was.

My brother, who was humble in his ways and keenly intelligent, was a man of few words. But he realized that he owed us all an explanation. He related that he had left Holland in May of 1940, riding his bike into Belgium. There, close friends had helped him through France, where other business relations had gotten him over the Pyrenees Mountains and into Spain.

In Spain Ben had contacted the Dutch embassy and indicated that he wanted to join the Allied army. After they had checked him out thoroughly, he was sent to England, where he was trained and later joined the Allied troops in the Princess Irene Brigade. He fought his way through Normandy. He was one of our libera-tors in the south of Holland, where he had been for one year. He had served as a translator—my brother spoke several languages fluently—and also worked in the intelligence units.

Ben told his story in a simple way, not making much ado about it. He finished by saying how enormously happy he was to find us, especially since his superior officer had said to him, "Listen, Cohen, don't expect to find any of your family members alive." Yet his in-tuition brought him to my oldest brother's store.

We stood there fascinated with my brother's story. But I knew that at some point we had to talk about what had happened to our mother and our other family members from Amersfoort. I dreaded having to relive that horrible evening when the Nazis picked up my mother and deported her. I simply could not bear to discuss that day of hell.

Felix held my hand and took over. He spoke about how things had gone terribly wrong for my mother and later for the aunt and uncle whom we all had loved so much. He told them how we had gotten married by Mr. Van Dam and that we had been the last couple married in that small synagogue. He discussed the many friends taken away by the Nazis, and he related the death of my Uncle Isse. Felix talked about Piet and the Hornsvelds. The people surrounding us, total strangers, occasionally shook their heads in disbelief. Some of them began to curse those "damned and cruel Germans."

A long time had passed, and then suddenly we heard loud cheering and shouting coming from the main street of the town. The Canadians had finally arrived in their cars and jeeps. My sister was the first to run out into the street with all of us following her and the crowd of people running behind us.

Coming to the main street, called De Lange Straat, a spectacle unfolded that I will never forget. There was no holding back any longer. The Canadians, in their impressive uniforms, looking healthy and well nourished, must have been overwhelmed. Young people literally stormed onto the cars and jeeps; flowers flew all over the streets. People surrounded the columns, throwing streamers, flags, cheering, waving, and becoming wild. At one point we could not even see the Canadians because everyone was jumping on their cars. We later heard a Canadian ask, "Are these the restrained Dutch?" The Dutch were expressing their exuberance.

I kept thinking, "How full of changes and uncertainties is life. One minute there is sadness, the next minute happiness. Everything seems to be intertwined." My thoughts went to all those who had been deported. What had happened to them? Were they coming back? When would we know? My thoughts then returned to Mr. Van Dam's words: "There is a time for crying, a time for laughing, a time for grief, and a time for joy. God brings everything to pass precisely at its time."

Epilogue

Mr. and Mrs. Hornsveld with us on one of their visits to the United States

Though the Germans had left my country a tremendous mess, the Dutch spirit was soaring. One of the first restorations was changing the streets back to their original names. On several occasions these changes were accompanied by religious ceremonies. All signs that the Germans so maliciously had put up to eliminate the Jewish population in Holland were removed, and all traffic and directional indicators in the German language were taken away.

After five years of war, destruction, terror, and starvation, the Dutch had a tremendous task ahead of them to rebuild their country. All laws that the German High Command had instituted during their occupation were immediately canceled. The cities and harbors had to be rebuilt, and food distribution had to be organized. The health and school systems had to be raised to meet prewar standards.

Food and clothing were brought to us in abundant quantities. The United States and Sweden were sending loads of food, clothing, and various items whose existence we had all but forgotten. Banners flew across Holland: Amerika Helpt (America Helps). The Jewish Joint Distribution Committee of America also set up depots to deliver kosher food, clothing, toiletries, shoes, and stockings. Even prayer books and other religious items were made available to us.

Memorial services were held in the various cities and towns for the many victims of the war, for the fallen heroes of the resistance, and for the Jewish citizens who had been so brutally deported and who had perished at the hands of the Nazis. A very special day was set aside on May 12, 1945, for the Jewish citizens who were still alive. According to the newspapers, out of approximately 140,000 Dutch Jews, only 6,000 had survived.

For the first time in all of the years of terror for the Jewish people of Holland, Shabbat services were held in makeshift synagogues—in ambulances donated by the Jewish population of England. These services were frequently attended by Canadian officers of the Jewish faith as well as members of the Princess Irene Brigade.

In spite of all I had been through, all I had witnessed over the dreadful years of the ruthless German occupation, I still entertained a flicker of hope that I would one day hear from my mother. It was too soon to contact the Red Cross, although we all tried hard to find information about our loved ones and what had happened to them.

Shortly after the liberation, the son of my sister's husband was brought back to Amersfoort from a concentration camp. He looked like a skeleton, almost unable to speak. It turned out that he and his sister had been picked up by the Germans and deported to Poland. His sister died in the camp.

We found out that my Aunt Sien and her younger son, Jacob, had survived; her older son, Simon, had ended up in the death camp of Auschwitz, the largest extermination camp established by Himmler in 1940. Simon, almost near death, had been liberated by the advancing Russian troops, who had dropped him off at Prague, fearing that he would die on the way. He was then sent by the Red Cross to the south of France, where they tried to bring him back to health. In 1946 they were able to return him to Holland.

My uncle perished in the death camp of Sobibor, and the same fate befell my relatives in Amersfoort, as well as other relatives and friends. Now we learned about the gas chambers and the many other atrocities to which the Germans had subjected the Jews. When we realized the magnitude of the German crimes orchestrated to reach their "Final Solution," our minds could not comprehend it. The shock was so immense that I could not bear thinking of how my mother had found her death.

The news that was broadcast from the crystal radio had never mentioned anything about the fate of the Jewish people in the concentration camps. Having gone through the war, I knew the mentality of the Germans but not to the extent of what I now was reading in the newspapers. What could possibly have brought the people of this so-called cultured nation to such hellish crimes?

After the war Felix and I contacted the Dutch Red Cross to find out where my mother had been, and indeed we learned that my mother had faced her death exactly the day that I heard her voice call my name.

In 1946 the official letter arrived from the Red Cross confirming that my mother and all other family members and friends that we had inquired about had perished in the gas chambers of Sobibor.

We immediately began to search out where exactly Sobibor was located. We learned that it had been one of the six extermination camps in Poland, and it was situated in a wooded area near a small village by the same name in the Lublin District. At the Wannsee Conference, held in January 1942, the Germans decided to speed up the extermination of the Jewish people, and in March 1942 they began construction work on this camp to prepare for mass extermination of all Jews.

By now we simply had to think about our future. Both the Brandsen and the Hornsveld families insisted that we stay with them for as long as we wanted. But we had to pick up the pieces of our lives and start all over. It was not easy. First we had to go to several different authorities to verify our true identities and to show proof of our time in hiding. The authorities were very helpful. Soon after, the resistance organization helped us locate a home. Through this organization Felix's family, who wanted to stay in Amersfoort, was allotted a home in this town.

Felix wanted to go back to Rotterdam. With all kinds of reference papers from the resistance, we qualified for a nice flat there. Once on our own, Felix immediately applied for Dutch citizenship, which he received in 1947.

The aftermath of our five-year ordeal was mind-boggling. Once we were settled in our flat in Rotterdam, we went back to Amersfoort to see if the many documents that we had collected over the years had been saved. First we went to the Brandsen home. After digging and digging in a particular spot in their yard, we found the two metal boxes and all of the documents and clippings in good condition.

From there we went to the Hornsvelds', where our diaries and other important papers remained in hiding places. We then went to Mrs. Kolkman's to look for the family photos, which my mother had so reverently saved and taken to Amersfoort. They were all in good condition as well. We were very grateful. It lifted my spirits to know that I had something from my past, especially photos from my mother, to cling to.

My sister and her husband, as well as my oldest brother and his wife, stayed in Amersfoort. Ies was able to start his business again in the same store.

In 1946 I became pregnant, but because the doctor could not make it to our home on time during my labor, our baby girl was still-born. In June 1946 Felix's sister Nel gave birth to their son, Eric.

Both Felix and I wanted to get out of Holland, for the memories weighed heavily on us. In August, Japan surrendered and everyone hoped for permanent peace in the world. But soon after, the Cold War began. We applied for a visa to go to America, but at that time there was a quota system for entrance into the United States because of the recently begun Cold War. It would take a long time, but with the help and sponsorship of Felix's two brothers, Hugo and Sam, who had lived in New York for a number of years and served in the American army, we hoped to get our papers to leave Holland.

Finally, in 1948 the American embassy furnished us with visas, and in April we left Holland to begin a new life in the United States. We again had to part with our families. It seemed as if we were always saying good-bye.

I managed to take all of our documents and war papers with me to America. They filled a large suitcase. Over the years I would look from time to time at that suitcase without opening it, knowing what dismal memories it held. On many occasions I was tempted to throw out the whole thing. But in later years I began to realize that those documents represented a piece of history that would be most important for the generations to come after us.

It wasn't until 1984 that I slowly began to sort through and file all of the war documents in chronological order. I translated certain documents into the English language. After several years of working on the project, Felix and I were able to donate our entire collection to the United States Holocaust Memorial Museum in Washington, D.C. The curator, who had come to our home for one entire day, was utterly amazed by such a large collection.

After Dina's death at a relatively young age, we invited Piet to our home in Newport Beach, California, which he visited many times. On one of his stays with us he insisted on giving us six precious bronze medals he received from the resistance organization in Holland for his courageous work during the war when he had saved many lives, including ours. We later donated these medals to the Holocaust Memorial Museum. Piet died of lung cancer in 1976.

Pa and Moe Hornsveld also stayed with us on several of their visits to America. Their two sons, Bertus and Hannie, immigrated to the United States in the 1950s and married their wartime girlfriends, now called Gerda and Hilde. Bertus earned his contractor's license in America and became a well-known and well-respected builder with his own company. To our deep sorrow, Bertus passed away of lung cancer in 1996. Hannie has his own thriving business in electrical appliances in Costa Mesa, California. The two brothers built Felix's and my home in Newport Beach; it is still beautiful and contemporary.

My prediction about Corrie Hornsveld's talent came to pass. She is now a noted Dutch painter and has received many commissions throughout the years. She is also registered with Sotheby's. On one of her visits to the States she presented us with a beautiful, delicately colored landscape painting, which adorns our dining room wall. It represents a tranquil scene in Amersfoort and portrays figures of young people on a canal on a crisp winter day. The bare branches of the trees surrounding the canal partially conceal the stucco home, which stands in silence. It embodies a world of haunting memories during the wartorn days spanning the five years of terror.

The four Brandsen girls remained in Holland and married, and some of them are already grandmothers. We remain in contact with each of the remaining sisters. To our great sorrow, Nel, the oldest, passed away unexpectedly.

After Kurt's mother passed away, Felix's family emigrated to South America, where they remained.

"Moltjeveer" (his real name was Mr. Van der Veer), whom we always visited on our trips to Holland, was very ill the last time we saw him. To our deep sorrow, he passed away soon after of lung cancer. His memory is a blessing to us.

I shall weep forever for the horrible fate of the millions of innocent men, women, children, and babies who were murdered by the German executioners in such abominable ways. It is my strong belief that with the destruction of the former centers of European Jewry, we must work to fulfill the dreams and goals of those whose voices are stilled forever.

We also must continue to strive for peace and understanding for all humankind.

Newport Beach, California, USA, June 2007

Piet Brandsen's first visit to America

Zentralstelle für jüdische
Auswanderung Amsterdam
Adama v. Scheltemaplein 1
Telefoon 97001

1

N⁰ 95396

OPROEPING!

Aan   L   No.

U moet zich voor eventueele deelname aan een, onder politietoezichtstaande, werk-
verruiming in Duitschland voor persoonsonderzoek en geneeskundige keuring naar het door-
gangskamp Westerbork, station Hooghalen, begeven.

Daartoe moet U op .... om .... uur

op de verzamelplaats .... aanwezig zijn

    Als bagage mag medegenomen worden:

        1 koffer of rugzak
        1 paar werklaarzen
        2 paar sokken
        2 onderbroeken
        2 hemden
        1 werkpak
        2 wollen dekens
        2 stel beddengoed (overtrek met laken)
        1 eetnap
        1 drinkbeker
        1 lepel en
        1 pullover
        handdoek en toiletartikelen

en eveneens marschproviand voor 3 dagen en alle aan U uitgereikte distributiekaarten met
inbegrip van de distributiestamkaart.
    De mee te nemen bagage moet in gedeelten gepakt worden.

a.   Noodzakelijke reisbehoeften
    daartoe behooren: 2 dekens, 1 stel beddegoed, levensmiddelen voor 3 dagen, toiletgerei,
    etensbord, eetbestek, drinkbeker,

b.   Groote bagage
    De onder b. vermelde bagage moet worden gepakt in een stevige koffer of rugzak,
    welke op duidelijke wijze voorzien moet zijn van naam, voornamen, geboortedatum
    en het woord „Holland".
    Gezinsbagage is niet toegestaan.
    Het voorgaande moet nauwkeurig in acht genomen worden, daar de groote bagage in
    de plaats van vertrek afzonderlijk ingeladen wordt.
    De verschillende bewijs- en persoonspapieren en distributiekaarten met inbegrip van
    de distributiestamkaart mogen niet bij de bagage verpakt worden, doch moeten,
    voor onmiddellijk vertoon gereed, medegedragen worden.
    De woning moet ordelijk achtergelaten en afgesloten worden, de huissleutels moeten
    worden medegenomen.
    Niet medegenomen mogen worden: levend huisraad.

K 372

The Summons

INFORMATIEBUREAU VAN
HET NEDERLANDSCHE ROODE KRUIS
OPSPORING JOODSCHE PERSONEN

TELEFOON 43066 · HEERENGRACHT 479 · AMSTERDAM C.

Nr. 1025

BIJLAGEN:

TYPE: J.M.G.   J. P. A. No.

BETREFT: Informatie

BIJ BEANTWOORDING DAGTEEKENING EN NUMMER
VAN DIT SCHRIJVEN AAN TE HALEN

30 Januari 1946

den Heer F.Levi,
Brussestraat 13a,
Rotterdam.

Mijnheer,

    In antwoord op Uw aanvrage van 17-12-'45 heb ik de eer
U het volgende te berichten:

	is op transport gesteld met bestemming, althans in de richting van:	datum
Aleida Cohen-van Beek geb. 23-7-80	Auschwitz	7-9-42
Flora Frank-van Beek geb. 8-9-78	Sobibor (Polen)	11-5-43
Jules Frank geb. 11-4-86	id.	id.
Ephraim de Haas geb. 28-11-87	Auschwitz	12-10-42
Carolina Salzer-Erle geb. 14-6-67	id.	id.
Bernhard Salzer geb. 24-5-63	id.	id.
Trude Hofman-Blum geb. 30-1-14	id.	31-8-42
Günther Hofmann geb. 26-4-07	id.	id.
Hertha Mannheimer geb. 6-5-91	Sobibor.	7-9-43

    Daaruit komt niet bij voorbaat vast te staan, dat ge-
zochten aldaar hun laatste verblijfplaats hebben gevonden. Immers
in vele gevallen werden gedeporteerden naar voorhands onbekende
stemming verder gevoerd. De ervaring leert ons echter, dat op
een uitzondering, vergeleken bij het geheel, na, de kans op te-
rugkeer van gezochten zeer gering moet worden geacht.

    Het onderzoek, hetwelk op grote moeilijkheden stuit, wordt
desniettemin voortgezet.

    Inmiddels verblijf ik

                         hoogachtend,
            HET NEDERLANDSCHE ROODE KRUIS
               de chef der Afdeeling
          Opsporing Joodsche Personen

*This is a copy of the letter we received from the Red Cross
confirming the death of my mother and other family members.*

This grievous lamentation by an unknown husband was found after the war. The Van Beeks brought it with them to America.

LONELINESS

Your lips
Which I have kissed so much
Your hair
So dark and tousled
Your heart
Your young and tender heart
On which I rested my head
  in gentle, loving passion.

Did it have to be this way
I ask within
For I do not know whether you
  died
How and when—so far away.

Are you in pain
Are you in hunger
What wanderings are left to us
Before we are together again
Oh, will we be together
Again?

That early spring morning
When you left our home
Wearing your white, thin blouse
How sunny and happy you were
For neither of us heard
The soft rustlings of death
Neither of us could see
The scepter of fate
The shadowy wings of forever

Flying over your face
That turned to me
Radiantly smiling
Then.
During all those fearsome nights
And days
It seemed I detected your brisk
Light steps
Walking our stairs
And then, nothing but a single
  letter
A dreaded form letter
Bearing your name, a stamp of
  Germany
The barrack number that became
  your home
And you asked for warm clothing.

My heart refused to break
Just then
Oh, not just then
For I saw you somewhere very far
Alone
Standing near a river
Was it beside the waters
  of Babylon
Wearing a slave's chain?

If I had Aladdin's wonderlamp
And the flying carpets of the sultan
And the caliphs

I would fly the clouds of memory
Until I might descend upon your
  camp
My arms to embrace you tightly
Never again to let you go
But to lift you to the skies
And the stars

To the islands of Epipsychidion,
Orpheus or Ogygia
To long forgotten shores
There to be together, my Calypso,
To kiss your hands
Which tended to our home so
  lovingly
And then
And then, kiss your dark and
  tousled hair.

Who knows whether we will see
  each other
Again
Is there but one purpose to the
  tortures
To our severed threads of life
That were woven for a shattered
  fragment
Of forever?

But then
To live without a shadow of hope
Is not enough
And so we cling in dream, my
  beloved,
You and I
To the dream that we shall return
To our paradise
The one given to me when I had
  you
Where the winds of love were soft
  and playful
Exotic beneath exquisite trees
Where you, whom I loved so
  deeply,
Shall again caress my tired head.

Our last kiss was swift
Too swift, too short
As farewells slipped away
In the union of our lips
Quickly, with a smile
So very quickly.

My heart aches for you
As I must ask:
How will our final kiss
Survive eternity?

The Singing Children of Bergen-Belsen

On Sunday night, May 27, 1945, the BBC broadcast an event from the concentration camp at Bergen-Belsen, Germany, where Dutch Jews had been transported during the Holocaust. On this occasion, a number of Dutch Jewish children who had survived their ordeal in the camp sang a Dutch folk song in honor of their liberators, the American and British armed forces. The event was of such great emotional impact to the reporters and soldiers that one American Jewish officer tried to express his feelings by writing the poem below, which was printed with great reverence in the Dutch newspapers in 1945. The last part of the poem contains the Jewish prayer of gratitude for life. In translation it means:

"Blessed are Thou, O Lord, our God, King of the Universe who has kept us in life, and has sustained us and enabled us to reach this season."

A few meters away from the dead, the horror, the fierce stench which
  Can never be forgotten by those who saw it,
  But will linger on forever,
And will bring fear to a soldier in the dark,
And will make him feel guilty should he once again be cheerful
Children are singing, innocent, as if they were celebrating a birthday,
They are singing in the camp of Bergen-Belsen
  For the soldiers who liberated them;
They sing a Dutch song, appropriate for the occasion:
  "May they live long, may they live long
    Gloria, Gloria"

Is it not a contrast that they sing while their parents have been killed?
We hear their children's voices, so pure, so clear,
But before their eyes, innocent and unknowing,

Must be such dreadful visions
That even a knowing man's voice would stop
And yet, those children, who shared this horror for weeks, months, years,
How can they sing so unshaken,
These young orphans of Bergen-Belsen, standing there neatly,
    As if in a classroom, where someone just celebrated his birthday
Singing in just the right tune:
    "May they live long, may they live long
        Gloria, Gloria"

Is it not strange that they should sing
With the little of what they remember from the past
Some songs perhaps, some memories,
Now, so hopelessly out of context
That it might be better to just forget;
Because, if death will shun away from them and if death
    Will be their companion no longer,
Their lives will become very bitter in a world where
    They have no home, no parents
And everyone is left to strangers, to care for them
And yet: they are singing in their loving voices, so sweet and pure
As only a child's voice can be ...
    "May they live long, may they live long
        Gloria, Gloria"

While above the camp of Bergen-Belsen the sky is blue
And again, the larks fly jubilantly up to heaven
Because the summer is near,
The children acquire perhaps from their own singing a force,
Which ages could not break
A special force, which gave strength to generations before them,
    And which has kept them alive:
Now, to the voices of these innocent children of Bergen-Belsen
    So sweet and brave, I add my own voice
First, a bit husky and subdued, and hesitatingly ...
But then I too sing ... May they live long, may they live long ...
    Baruch Atah Adaonay Eloheynu Melech Ha-Olam,
    Shehecheyanu, Ve'kiyemanu, Ve'higiyanu Lazman Hazeh ...